THE WORLD OF
MUSICAL INSTRUMENT MAKERS:
A GUIDED TOUR

THE WORLD OF
MUSICAL INSTRUMENT MAKERS:
A GUIDED TOUR

William Laskin

Photographs by Brian Pickell

MOSAIC PRESS

Oakville — New York — London

CANADIAN CATALOGUING IN PUBLICATION DATA

Laskin, Grit
    The world of musical instrument makers

ISBN 0-88962-349-X

1. Musical instruments – Makers – Canada.
I. Pickell, Brian.   II. Title.

HD9999.M83C35 1987   681'.8'0922   C87-094539-4

Published by Mosaic Press, P.O. Box 1032, Oakville, Ontario, L6J 5E9, Canada. Offices and warehouse at 1252 Speers Rd, Unit 10, Oakville, Ontario, L6L 5N9, Canada.

Published with the assistance of the Canada Council and the Ontario Arts Council.

Copyright ©William Laskin, 1987
Design by Rita Vogel
Typeset by Michael J. O'Leary
Printed and bound in Hong Kong

ISBN 0-88962-349-X cloth

MOSAIC PRESS:

In the United States:
Riverrun Press Inc., 1170 Broadway, Suite 807, New York, N.Y., 10001, U.S.A..

In the U.K.:
John Calder (Publishers) Ltd., 18 Brewer Street, London, W1R 4AS, England.

Cover Photographs

MASA-TOSHI INOKUCHI   RAAD

MICHAEL SCHREINER   DAVID WREN

(back cover)

WILLIAM LASKIN

Brian Pickell's eighteen years of professional photography have taken him three times to the Soviet Union, to China, Japan, Cuba and the countries of continental Europe. His first book was '27 *Days In September*', the official photographic history of the first Canada/Russia hockey series. As a freelancer, his work has appeared in *Toronto Life* and *Time Canada* as well as being regularly seen in the *Toronto Star*. Working in journalism adds the third generation to a family tradition. Both his father and grandfather were publisher-editors of weekly newspapers. Also, for seven years, Brian played music professionally, touring and recording several albums with a band he helped form. He still plays music part time and lives with his wife and daughter in Toronto.

William Laskin, a.k.a. Grit Laskin, has been a professional guitar maker for close to sixteen years. His instruments receive the highest praise from players as far afield as Japan, the United States, Britain and Europe. He has lectured and demonstrated his craft in schools, museums music camps, on radio, television and in films. He is also a performing and recording musician, known for his multi-instrumentalist skills as well as his compositions. When he is not in his workshop or on stage, he is either writing articles for Canadian and American craft magazines, patenting an invention, helping to plan international guitar festivals or curating musical instrument exhibitions. He lives and works in Toronto, his favourite city.

TABLE OF CONTENTS

SECOND GALLERY

ACKNOWLEDGEMENTS

There were many individuals and organizations who gave freely of their time and assistance in the making of this book — not the least of whom were the instrument makers themselves.

Deserving of special thanks are my good friends, Fern Rubinstein for her valuable editorial suggestions, Brian Pickell for his keen photographer's eye, publisher Howard Aster for his unfaltering belief in the value of this project and especially to my wife Judith without whose ideas and support this book simply could not have been written.

I also gratefully acknowledge the assistance of the Canada Council, the Ontario Arts Council and the Woodlawn Arts Foundation of Toronto.

FOREWORD

If you are like myself, a visit to a gallery or museum becomes a most enjoyable learning experience when a guide, a docent or a pre-recorded tape provides the missing information, piques our curiosity with relevant facts and anecdotes and brings an inanimate object to life.

At my wife Judith's suggestion, I have assumed the role of guide to lead you through an exhibition of work by Toronto's present day musical instrument makers. Since there has never been a show quite like this, our plan called for an imaginary show assembled in an imaginary gallery as the setting for actual instruments from existing artisans.

As I pause before each instrument my capacity as guide calls, appropriately, for my telling of that instrument maker's story and describing their work in finer detail. The conversational tone intrinsic to guided tours helps to keep the flow of supplementary information on construction processes, historical developments, acoustics, etc. accessible to both the musician and non-musician, the maker and non-maker.

Joining us and comprising our tour group will be as varied a collection of people as one might find attending a musical instrument exhibition. Their variety will be reflected by the questions they pose as we proceed. From the moment you begin reading the introduction, you become the final member of that fictitious group.

INTRODUCTION

I would like to welcome you to this exhibition of work by musical instrument makers. My name is William Laskin (Grit to my friends) and I am the exhibition's curator. What you are about to see is the first show of its kind ever assembled.

I am sure that many of you do not realize that metropolitan Toronto is the *handmade musical instrument centre of Canada and one of the major centres on the continent.* We have over thirty professional makers of all types of instruments in this city and almost all of them are represented in this show.

Toronto is also host to dozens of devoted amateur builders. Of these, some are self-taught, but many acquired their skills at one of the various instrument-making courses offered around town. The Ontario College of Art has its 'Stringed Instrument Construction' classes; the Twelfth Fret shop teaches electric guitar making; as does Joe Lado; Michael Schreiner takes students in his own shop and some Metro high schools offer night courses in constructing violins and guitars.

But for this show I was interested only in professional builders. Their inclusion was based on the following criteria: the craftspeson pursued his or her trade full time, for the major portion of their income (as is the case in most instances) and/or their work is recognized to be of the highest professional standards by the music world.

There are some instrument repair establishments in Toronto whose work is of exceptional quality and whose valued supplementary role I acknowledge. In their employ are craftspeople who occasionally build an instrument and often do it very well but the full story of them and their respective firms will have to be told another time.

This show has not been juried. Since as I've explained, it is an exhibition of professional work that has withstood the judgements of a discriminating and finicky market, it seemed unnecessary to pass judgement a second time. It was only for lack of space that I was forced to limit most makers to submitting a maximum of two instruments even though some build many different types.

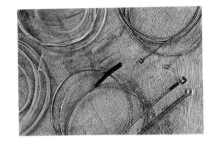

I assembled this exhibition to show the world outside of musicians' and makers' circles what has emerged under their unsuspecting noses. Within the last two decades, handmaking musical instruments in Toronto has grown into a firmly established and still expanding, small-scale industry. This city is witnessing the irreversible development of a handmade instrument tradition — one that is comprised, I might add, of unusually high standards of work.

A question that kept arising during the planning for this guided tour was: why does Toronto have such a high proportion of instrument makers? Unlike Cremona, Italy, Paris, France or Barcelona, Spain, Toronto's history contains only a few prominent instrument-making events.

Between 1855 and 1930 there were at least twenty-six piano and organ manufacturers in Toronto. Familiar names like Heintzman, Mason and Risch, Nordheimer and R.S.Williams are just a few from among that thriving group of manufacturers. However after the turn of the century and continuing through to the depression, almost all of these companies either went out of business, left the city for cheaper premises in nearby towns or became distribution and repair services. Alone out of this group of piano makers, R.S.Williams, himself an apprentice of a Toronto maker of melodeons, William Townsend, manufactured string instruments as well; mandolins, banjos, guitars and violins.

Prior to the demise of this side of the Williams company — which petered out by the 1930s — an Austrian violin maker, George Heinl, was recruited to Toronto. Heinl later established a reputable studio of his own which still exists in the hands of his grandsons. Regrettably though, their present instrument work is mostly confined to repairs and restoration.

One other violin maker, George Kindness, whose business also remains with us primarily as a repair and retail sales concern, was a fellow employee of Mr. Heinl at the Williams factory.

The Whaley Royce company, founded in 1888 and continued after 1920 to make brass instruments and drums, is today but a retailer and distributor of electric, electronic and band instruments.

In the 1920s a violin maker named Friedrich Haanel was popularly considered to be Toronto's best. Unfortunately he left us, — for Philadelphia!

Early in the next decade, another violin maker, Piet Molenaar, opened a studio and though still with us, he has recently retired.

By the close of the first half of this century, records indicate that there was little other instrument making of consequence in Toronto. We compared poorly to the healthier, flourishing scenes in Montreal and Quebec City. Of the working craftspeople known to have been trained by our earliest violin and piano makers or their descendants, most make their living today from repairing instruments, not building them.

This state of affairs remained essentially unchanged until the 1960s, when dramatic changes took place. In that decade, an unprecedented number of young people were searching for new lifestyles and many of them turned to craftswork. Although the making of instruments demanded long-term dedication if it was to be mastered, it began to attract its share of devotees.

The sixties marked, as well, the beginning of Toronto's rapid cultural growth. That decade and the 1970s saw Toronto blossom into the arts centre of Canada. In a country, when a centre develops, it acts as a magnet drawing to itself more and more like-minded people. In Canada, with our thinly spread population, we simply do not have enough people for Numerous major centres of any one thing. But a single and highly visible centre sustains an irresistible attraction. Toronto's emergence signalled to the entire country that it was here, in 'Hog-town', that Canada's theatre, music and visual arts were prospering.

Attracted to the musical vitality of the city, the German guitarmaker Edgar Monch arrived in 1965 and was followed in 1974 by the New York based, Hungarian viola maker Otto Erdesz. Unlike Toronto's earlier instrument makers, these two men passed on their knowledge to apprentices who, as professional makers themselves have taught and influenced many others. (Of these, guitarmaker Jean Larrivée is deservedly the most well known). Thus, the foundation for a truly established makers' community was provided.

My intention, with this exhibition, is to enable you to experience the visible proof of this community's vibrancy. By that means, you will come to know a measure of the musical instrument maker's world.

Now, as I take you through the show, I'll be stopping at each separate exhibit to tell you about the individual maker and his or her work. At any time, if you have questions, no matter how technical or how silly you think them to be, please ask.

So, let's move into the first gallery where we shall begin with the Walke brothers.

FIRST GALLERY

1 Violins, Violas, Modern and Baroque Bows.
Gregory and Bernard Walke

Since most people more readily associate handmade instruments with the violin family — some because they've heard the name Stradivari, others because their great uncle built a few violins — I've placed this violin and viola at the start of the exhibition.

With Stradivari's first "classical" model violin around the year 1700, Cremona, Italy was the setting for the culmination of 150 years of the instrument's development. Stradivari was following the lead of Andrea Amati, the father of the enduring 'Cremona School', and Amati's grandson Nicolo. All three of these makers, like those who have come since, could and did make each instrument of the violin family.

In this grand tradition is Gregory Walke, born in 1952, a native Torontonian working out of a basement workshop in the west end of Metro.

Although he is labelled simply a "violin maker", Gregory has chosen to represent himself here with this pair of immaculate but differing instruments. The back, ribs*, and necks are built with North American curly maple. For the sound-boards*, he used Sitka spruce from Alaska, and the fingerboards* are of ebony.

The colour of the instrument is generally not the wood's natural hue. Like most makers of the violin family of instruments, Gregory stains his varnish. He applies, then hand rubs this tinted oil (or spirit) varnish in the traditional manner known as french polishing*, building up thin layer after thin layer until the smooth shine evolves. This process takes him an entire week for each instrument.

While working as a biologist, his first field of study, Gregory wanted to do something less academic and more practical with his life. He already had some woodworking experience making toys and the like, but a keen interest in Irish fiddling, which took him to Ireland, steered him to violin making and playing.

He built his first violin on his own while searching in vain for an apprenticeship. Then, in May 1979, he began a two-year period of intense studying at the Welsh School of Instrument Making and Repair in Wales.

In the last few years, since his return to Toronto, classical violin teachers here and in Ottawa have spread word of his work throughout southern Ontario. With the superior craftsmanship evident in these instruments, his future and reputation as a master builder is assured.

It takes Gregory two to three weeks to do the woodworking on one instrument...a question?
DEBORAH: Yes. I was told that the arch of the top and back is created by pressing the wood into that shape. Is that true?

No. That is definitely NOT true. The tops and backs are carved from a thick, solid piece of wood using gouges, tiny finger planes, sandpaper and a lot of elbow grease.

It's a coincidence that you asked that particular question because carving the plates*, as they are sometimes called is one of Gregory's favourite moments in the building process. Did you have another question?
DEBORAH: I'm curious...Did you call the wood on the back CURLY maple?

I did. But it is also known as flamed maple, tiger maple or fiddleback maple.
DEBORAH: What makes some maple curly and some not?

The formation of the wavy or curly grain is a deviation from normal growth patterns by the wood's longitudinal cell structure. Although it is an abnormal feature, the curl figure occurs with enough frequency that the "stricken" wood is fairly easy to obtain — albeit at inflated prices.

When the surface of curly maple is smoothed, as in this violin back, the deviated cells intersect the face at various angles. As a consequence, when reflecting light, they produce the two-dimensional "tiger-stripe".

Now, if you'll just shift to the right a few feet you will encounter two bows made by Gregory Walke's twin brother, Bernard.

The simple aesthetic lines of a well-made bow conceal the precise and exacting work necessary in its construction. Bowmaking is considered to be a skill entirely separate from building the instrument with which it is used. Hence, there are few violin makers who regularly make

GREGORY WALKE

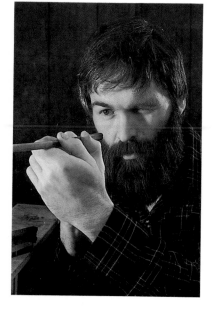

BARNARD WALKE

equally good bows and vice versa.

What convenience and good fortune then for Gregory to have his brother Bernard making bows and sharing the same shop. To be fair, Bernard began his bowmaking not by coincidence or the luck of fate but primarily at his brother's urging.

Bernard did, however, share his brother's interest in Irish fiddling. It too inspired him to take up instrument building. Once Bernard had the bug to try his hand at bowmaking, initial inquiries brought him to Peter Mach, a bowmaker in southern Ontario.

I'm getting slightly ahead of myself. It's important to know that during a period of unemployment Bernard took advantage of his available time to study log house construction and, through various kinds of "stone work", gain basic masonry skills. When he added a year of furniture making in Switzerland to his growing store of abilities, Bernard emerged well skilled as a renovator.

You can appreciate then his stroke of luck at finding a bowmaker whose house needed major renovation! For approximately two years Bernard worked on Peter Mach's house in exchange for being taught the skills of bowmaking.

It has been almost six years since Bernard finished his apprenticeship and at a pace of three bows every couple of weeks, he has completed over 250. He builds bows for all the violin family of instruments and the related baroque viol family.

Of the bows, we are looking at, two are 'modern' — their shaping and the materials utilized in their construction precluding their use on baroque or Renaissance instruments — and two are, indeed, baroque. The main portion of each modern bow is made from a wood called pernambuco, the frogs*, are ebony inlaid with ivory, silver and mother of pearl, the handgrips are leather wound over with silver wire and lastly is of course, the horsehair. In contrast, a baroque bow is traditionally built from snakewood with a cho-

Bernard inserting balled end of horsehair into bow tip.

*see glossary

ice of just one other material, bone, ebony or ivory, for the frog.

A bow's main shaft may be octagonally shaped, as are Bernard's, or round depending on the aesthetic sense of its maker. Neither shape has an advantage over the other. But whichever shape the wood is ultimately given, a shellac and linseed oil finish is most commonly used to protect it.

1

2

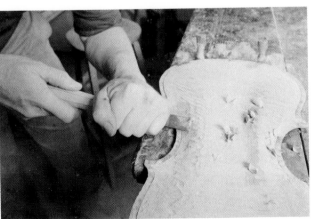

3

4

CARVING A VIOLA BACK

1. John Newton, a viola/violin maker who we shall meet later in the tour, demonstrated some of the stages in the making of a viola back. Here the two book-matched wedges of maple are selected.
2. The two pieces are glued and clamped together.
3. After the back has been cut roughly to shape, the arch is achieved by removing excess wood with chisels.
4. Tiny hand planes smooth out the jagged chisel marks prior to sanding. The same process, using gouge chisels, is repeated on the underside of the back. Specially designed calipers are used to confirm thicknesses during that stage.

SAMUEL: I've had bows with white horsehair and some with both white and black. Is there a difference?

Not really. It has always been a simple matter of colour preference. Horsehair that is naturally white is considered superior and a maker must pay accordingly — as much as $250 per pound. Often, the cheaper black hair is bleached to improve its status, but the hair's colour alone does not affect its playability.

SAMUEL: Does the quantity matter?

Once again — a qualified no. Whether thickly or thinly bundled, the overall quantity of hair is in response to the individual maker's or player's wants. For a given bow, Bernard uses nothing more mysterious than sight and feel to judge the necesary hair quantity.

SAMUEL: One last question...How is the horsehair held in place?

To begin with, the hair ends are gathered and wrapped with either wire or cotton string. They are then dabbed with rosin and burned slightly to form a little ball. The balled ends can then be easily gripped and wedged out of sight into both the tip and frog.

Another hidden but more critical aspect to a bow's construction is the balancing — a task Bernard finds particularly satisfying. It seems there must always be a physical balance point on a bow within one inch of a spot 11 to 12 inches from the frog. Occasionally tiny weights are added into the tip or a different stiffness of wood utilized if a lighter or heavier feel is demanded by a player.

One more surprising fact. To achieve the accurate straightness it must have when under playing tension, a bow is heat bent as many as fifteen different times!

Now, I thought I saw someone else with a question.

DEBORAH: How much do bows like these cost?

These bows sell for just under $1,000. One could however spend many thousands of dollars on a bow if one so chose.

I spotted that knowing nod ma'am. If you're familiar with bow prices you must be a musician.

LOUISE: I am. I compose and play the piano but my eldest daughter is a viola player and we've been shopping for a better instrument and a better bow.

Then you know what one can pay for a good musical instrument.

I'd like us to move to the next exhibit now. It's on the opposite side of the entranceway. We'll be looking at the silver and gold flutes that have been tantalizing us since we first stepped into the gallery.

2 Concert Flutes
Jack and Mara Goosman

DOUG: "My brother had a flute."

Oh?

DOUG: "Ya, he said it was made outa steel and covered in chrome. I told 'im no way but then he says he'll prove it. He never proved it though 'cause I sat on it. By mistake like and it bent into a curve like this . . . Anyway if it was steel it wouldn'ta bent like that would it? That's my question."

No, I guess it wouldn't have.

These flutes however would fare no better from being sat on. They are fashioned from eight different sizes of tubing, flat stock and rectangular wire of solid gold and silver. The composition of the entire flute from highly valued metals, even platinum on occasion, makes for a costly but superior instrument.

Jack Goosman, his wife Mara and until just recently, one helper, Yutaka, spend an average of six weeks bringing one flute to completion. In their workshop, an upper floor section of a pleasant old downtown industrial building, they carry on the skills Jack acquired and developed in the demanding environment of the Verne Q. Powell shop in Boston, Massachusetts.

Jack and Mara met while both were music students—flute majors—at different universities. Jack was studying with the first flutist of the Pittsburgh Symphony, while the future Ms. Goosman studied in Boston. Jack, being mechanically inclined and needing a job, landed a spot in the Powell establishment in 1971. Within two years, he rose from being a 'padder', the job of applying the corks, rings and pads of the keys on a flute a process that now takes Mara a week to ten days to complete to a maker of 'head joints', the crucial mouthpiece section.

After two years, Jack left the Powell shop, But during that time he had developed such skill for the precise work in a *head joint* that he was asked to build this segment of the instrument for them even after leaving.

Soon afterward, Jack and Mara chose to emigrate to Canada. Partially due to their need to distance themselves from the ever present rivalries among the makers and players in the American flute community, a common enough occurrence in musical and other creative circles anywhere. Not only were they attracted to Toronto's clean subways, but the location allows them to be independent from, but still part of, the larger flute communities in the U.S.

Jack had no difficulty setting up a repair business, because of his training in the shop of one of the world's most respected flute makers. Two years later, at the urging of a player willing to put up the funds, he built his first flute. From that start over ten years ago, Jack, with the help of his wife and Yutaka, has maintained a production of approximately twenty instruments per year and has built up an international clientele from Japan, Australia, Europe and North America.

Yutaka Chiba

Silver tubing, partially completed flutes and templates for fingerhole placement from the Goosman workshop.

James Galway, considered to be one of the two leading flutists in the world, owns a Goosman instrument and believes it to be the best handmade flute he has ever played.

The modern classical concert flute that emerged from the woodwind family of instruments has been fabricated from silver and other metals since the middle of the last century. It was in 1847 that Theobald Boehm, a goldsmith and professional flutist from Munich, Germany, presented to the world his first cylindrical silver flute. His monumental impact as 'the king of 19th century woodwind engineers' distinguished him from the many other talented craftsman of his day, and even now the modern flute is considered the embodiment of the 'Boehm system'.

That first instrument, with its modified key and fingering systems, and the succeeding ones which received subtler and more innovative refinements, have become the concert instruments still in use. To modern flute makers, in addition to the perfection of craftsmanship, there still remains the further refining and setting of scales — a task which the Goosmans pay particular heed.

Yes? Go ahead....

SUSAN: How thick is the tube part?

It's only 14/1,000 of an inch thick on the silver flute and less, 11/1,000 or 12/1,000 on the gold. Delicate but durable aptly describes these and, I suppose, all superior instruments regardless of type.

The necessary care that these concert flutes receive in their manufacture is exemplified by the month-long effort spent in hand shaping the keys — parts that could, if desired, be stamped out by machine.

One final point. There is no finish on these or most other flutes. The brilliant gleam of the metals has been achieved solely from two very careful polishings.

I'll step aside for a moment to let you have a closer look before I take you to our next stop for something completely different.

Follow me please, to the exhibit beside Bernard Walke's bows where you'll find two of the most recognizable instruments from the world of popular music: an electric guitar and an electric bass.

Five people under the collective name *The Twelfth Fret — Guitarists' Pro Shop* build 30 or 40 guitars of any and all styles, every year. Owners Dan Charman and Grant MacNeill with three main assistants, Gordon Barry, Pat Keenan and Alain Brouard, not only build electric guitars but also teach electric guitar building. They maintain one of the most reputable instrument repair facilities in the city and run a modest retail business.

Relying on the electronics and not the acoustics to produce the sounds, electric guitars can be and are made in almost every shape imaginable. The Twelfth Fret folks have built everything from a guitar in the shape of a smile to the double neck bass we have here. If you look carefully at this bass guitar, you'll spot the reason for the two necks. One neck has frets as usual but the other is fretless*, allowing a player the feel of an acoustic string bass.

Don't let the fire engine red lacquer finish on one of their other guitars surprise you. According to Grant, this is a typical colour for electric guitars. They have also finished instruments in every conceivable shade, including the pastel blues and oranges popular in the 1950s and "black, for the rock stars" as Grant puts it.

Grant, the musician, with some training as a piano repairer/tuner, and Dan, the co-owner of the Conception Case Co. which built flight cases for musical instruments, became a team and began using their self-taught skills in June of 1977. It was then that they first set up their store and repair shop on Kingston Road, where it remains. Although they constructed their first electric instrument around that time, it was not until three years later that guitar building became the significant part of their work. "As repairmen we could and did see every single design error (in electric guitars) and it made us want to avoid them and build the better guitar. It was only the secure money in repairs that held us back."

Gordon Barry, the one employee most involved with the shops' instrument construction is a luthier in his own right. Since 1984, he has been dividing his time equally between the *Twelfth Fret* and his own coach house workshop where he produces numerous models of steel string guitars and on occasion, something unusual like a Yugoslavian Brache. Gordon spent five years in Jean Larrivée's west coast workshop before being drawn to Toronto and its "thriving instrument scene". It was here that he sought and found, with the *Twelfth Fret*, the experience in repairwork he wanted, rounding out his skills. One day, I'm sure, will see Gordon working full time in his own shop.

TWELVTH FRET

Twelvth Fret custom built double neck electric bass made from walnut, maple and Macassar ebony with E.M.G. electronics. 131.5cm. x 34.5cm.

*see glossary

The World of Musical Instrument Makers

Gordon Barry, of the Twelvth Fret shop, holding a Yugoslavian Brache he recently completed. Hanging just behind him and to the right is one of his guitars.

Of the estimated 200 instruments the *Twelfth Fret* shop has made to date, a full half of them have been entirely customized instruments, built part by part exactly to the player's needs and desires. They use maple for the necks and choose either black walnut, mahogany, white ash or red cedar for the bodies. Fifty percent of their guitars are constructed in such a way that the wood for the neck runs continuously through the length of the body. The other fifty percent are made with necks that bolt to the body in the manner that the Fender Electrical Instrument Co. in the U.S. originated and has been marketing since 1948. Leo Fender co-invented the solid body electric guitar almost simultaneously with two other Californians. I'll describe the electric guitar's origins in more detail later in the tour.

The bodies of these guitars and almost all

electrics are solid woods with the recesses for the electronics, wiring and pickups routed* and drilled away.

Yes?

DEBORAH: You mentioned earlier that electric guitars produce sound by electronics.

Right.

DEBORAH: Well, how does that actually work? Do the pickups really pick up the sound or is it just a name they're given?

Alright, a good question. I'll explain what a pick-up does and let you be the judge as to whether it is really picking up the sound or not.

The magnetic pickups on guitars of this style are simply a coil of fine copper wire wrapped around a magnet or set of magnets. When a steel string vibrates through the created magnetic field, it causes the field to fluctuate. This induces the magnetic lines of force to cut through the many layers of wire causing in turn a voltage to be produced which is fed through an amplifier.

DEBORAH: And the amplifier is connected to the box with the speakers?

Exactly.

Let's step back across the room to what will be our fourth stop on the tour. It's there you'll discover two more guitars but ones that are a world apart from these electrics, as you'll soon see.

*see glossary

4 Classical Guitars, Multi-string Guitars
Sergei De Jonge

Have any of you seen a guitar like this one? I didn't think so. The reason is that there are few guitars like this in existence. In the multi-string family, this one, with seventeen individual strings, is stretching the limits of the guitar as we know it. Its maker, Sergei De Jonge, has also built seven, eight, ten and fifteen string classical guitars in addition to the plain, ordinary, old-fashioned six-string style like the other guitar he has on display here. Some of the extra strings are, as you can see, in a position over the wider fingerboard where they can be fretted and played. The remaining strings that reach to the tuning mechnanisms beyond the edge of the neck are played either for the open notes, as drone strings, or employed solely for their sympathetic vibrations.

The well-known guitarist Narciso Yepes, who began the serious multi-string idea with a ten string, gave this hybrid style of guitar legitimacy and respect.

Sergei has been involved with guitar making since early 1971. About a year and a half previous to that he saw a television special about the avant-garde classical guitar maker in Collingwood, Ontario, Pat Lister, and Sergei realized that with little spare cash, the only way he'd ever own a good guitar would be to make himself one. He abruptly quit teacher's college and guitar lessons at Eli Kassner's academy in Toronto to begin hanging out and observing in the shop of guitar maker Jean Larrivée. Sergei spent close to a year with Jean, during which time he made his first guitar, and then a further eleven months

with Pat Lister, his original inspiration. For the next five years, until 1978, Sergei worked on and off at guitar making — one year producing close to sixty instruments, another year, as other pursuits drew his attention from the shop, making only a few. Since then, Sergei has been producing an average of thirty guitars annually. He is assisted by Steve Leithwood, a man he trained, who is becoming a builder in his own right.

Both of the guitars we see have Brazillian rosewood for the back and sides of the body, cedar for the tops, mahogany and ebony for the neck and fingerboard respectively. Although these are traditional materials for superior guitar construction, Sergei, always the adventurous one, has used exotic woods like coco-bolo, pauferro, padauk or ebony for the bodies of the guitars and various spruces, redwood or Ontario white pine for the tops.

MICHAEL: How are the sides shaped?

There are a number of ways to bend wood. Yes, the sides of guitars, violins and the like are bent. They are not cut from a solid piece as some people suspect.

The sides for a guitar, at a thickness of 2 to 2.5 millimetres, can be boiled for twenty minutes, after which they are so pliable, they can be coaxed into shape and clamped to a mold, or they can be bent, essentially dry, over a heated pipe. Sergei uses the latter method which, although more difficult, leaves the bent side ready for use immediately as the shaping is completed.

SERGEI DE JONGE

1

2

BENDING A GUITAR SIDE

1. Sergei beginning to bend one rosewood side. It starts as a flat strip (note the second side that lays on the bench) and is shaped over a round metal pipe which has a heating element mounted inside. Steve Leithwood can be seen working in the background.
2. As the wood takes its shape, constant reference is made to the contours of the mould.

3. The bent side is reaching its final shape.
4. With few simple adjustments on the bending iron, the overbent lower bout curve will be brought to shape and the first side will be finished.

Sergei De Jonge 17-string cutaway classical guitar. Rosewood, mahogany, cedar, ebony 137.5cm. x 37.7cm.

3

4

Sergei has been in Canada since he was four years old. In 1953, his family emigrated here from The Hague in Holland. In 1977, he returned to his birthplace for a year, taking various woodworking jobs but continued his guitarmaking, albeit at a reduced level.

Sergei describes himself as someone who can't remain in one spot for too long and insists he doesn't know where the future may find him. It might be Holland, Nova Scotia or China. But for the near future, Toronto is home.

We have much still to see so I'd like to continue our brisk pace and take us back to the north wall of the gallery where we began. There we'll see a third and different kind of guitar, an acoustic steel string.

5 Steel String Guitars
David Wren

Between the two common types of acoustic guitars are many obvious differences, especially when seen side by side. The most evident is the larger and deeper body of the steel string. As well, its neck is narrower at the nut* than a classical and is joined to the body at the 14th fret instead of the 12th.

A classical guitar is strung with three nylon strings on the treble and three metal-wound-over-nylon on the bass with a resulting pull on the bridge of approximately 90 pounds. A steel string is strung with two steel treble strings and usually four bronze-wound-over-steel basses that exert approximately 150 pounds of pull.

Owing to the increased tension on a steel string, the woods of the body are thicker, the bracing* on the underside of the top is heavier and there is, of necessity, a metal rod of some type inserted in the neck to help it resist the pull of the strings.

Some guitar makers build both classical and steel string models, but since each type has its own idiosyncrasies of construction and acoustic responses, many prefer to specialize. David Wren, an exceptionally talented craftsman, is a maker solely of steel string guitars and is responsible for this beauty I've been referring to.

In 1971, David was a working commercial artist when he registered for a guitar making course in the wood working shop of a Metro high school. He built his first guitar there, a classical, oddly enough, with supplies that came, ironically, from the man to whom he would be apprenticed only one year later. From the beginning of 1973, David was coming to Jean Larrivee's workshop on Mt. Pleasant Road every evening after work and staying into the early morning hours. After six months of this routine, David decided to work full time with Jean and make guitar building his career.

Four years later, David set up his own shop. He has been building instruments, almost without interruption, ever since. I said instruments, plural, for a reason. David has made a few arch-top mandolins through the years and more recently has introduced a unique small-bodied, semi-electric, arch-top guitar (more about arch-tops later in the tour). He now builds, in addition, a limited but ever increasing number of solid body electric guitars. However, despite the various styles of guitars he enjoys building, his major preference to date seems to remain the flat top steel string such as these.

Speaking of this one, it's built primarily of Brazilian rosewood, mahogany, ebony and German spruce. I suspect that soon I'll not have to tell you which wood is used for which part. You're beginning to know. Just in case I'm still one step ahead of you, the rosewood is for the back and sides of the body, the spruce is the top, the black wood of the fingerboard and bridge is the ebony and I'll let you guess where the mahogany is.

DAVID WREN

David Wren insetting abalone shell pieces into routed groove surrounding soundhole.

The World of Musical Instrument Makers

ALAIN: Sir? Mr. Laskin?

Yes?

ALAIN: What's the blue stuff on the edges?

Great question. We haven't run across this material before now. These are strips of abalone shell — a shell that is physically similar to mother-of-pearl but more colourful. The abalone strips are about an inch long and David places them one at a time into a precisely gauged channel left between the rosewood and maple strips of the edge binding. If you'll look carefully — come up closer, it's alright — you can see where each little piece ends and the next begins.

While our youngest tour member scrutinizes the inlay, I'd like to mention that David is a native Torontonian and has been a guitar player since his high school days. But he has, through his years as a luthier, added a smattering of fiddle, mandolin, banjo and dulcimer playing to his musical repertoire.

David has set up one of this city's most

David Wren steel string guitar with abalone shell strip inlay. Brazillian rosewood, German spruce, ebony, mahogany. Body; 49.5cm. x 37.1cm.

pleasant basement workshops, where, in addition to guitar building, he occasionally restores guitars and even manages some cabinet work. Having built, as well, objects as varied as a full-sized loom and a celtic harp, it is obvious this very able guitar maker has never shied from any challenge.

If gently goaded into choosing one high point in his instrument making career, David would most likely describe a lumber buying trip to the docks of New York City he made shortly after his apprenticeship. With Jean Larrivee and, it so happened, myself, David found the wood dealers, the tool suppliers, New York itself and the wide new world of the guitarmaker that they represented to be a most delicious deviation from his suburban "white bread" (to use his words) upbringing.

I find it easy to agree with David that the immediate impressions he had upon starting into a new and fascinating career are those that remain the most vivid.

My own apprenticeship, for that is how I too learned the trade, began in the upper floor of a two-storey, midtown Toronto industrial building. My teacher had only just established this particular shop, his first outside of his home's basement. The shop inhabited the southeast wing of the building and was almost directly above the seating area for a new live theatre stage that was itself just being completed downstairs. This was the Tarragon, soon to become an innovative, nationally known theatre but at the time, for us, it was only an inconvenience.

If we were working late, as we usually did, and if there happened to be an evening performance, which there usually was, we had to refrain from using any stationary or hand power tools. The noise carried below. As that would often prevent us from getting on with the work at hand, my teacher and I would have no choice but to settle ourselves into the rear of the shallow lighting booth and watch performances for free. It was a hardship that we somehow managed to live with!

But enough of my rambling.

The next instrument I want to show you is not a guitar but is not very different from one. I'll give you a clue: its name is the root of the french word for a maker of stringed instruments

26

6 Lutes
Bruce Duncan

I can tell that most of you recognize this instrument. The word that was your clue is 'luthier', (pronounced: loo-tee-ay) and hence this instrument's name, the lute.

These were made by Bruce Duncan, one of the youngest makers in the show but one whose workmanship is beyond his years. On one he used curly sycamore, a European soft maple, for the strips that make up the bowl, as it's called, Swiss pine for the top, walnut for the neck and ebony for the fingerboard. On the other, the bowl is hard maple, the neck beech.

An unusual characteristic of the lute that separates it from modern fretted instruments is the use of gut string tied around the neck to act as frets. That has remained the tradition even though the frets have to be replaced every three or four months under full-time playing conditions.

The lute is an extremely lightweight instrument. Let me place this in your hands ma'am and you'll realize what I mean by lightweight. The top has areas as thin as 1 millimetre, and the strips, or more correctly, the ribs of the bowl are only slightly thicker. For Bruce, the most pleasurable stage in lute building is carving the rose, the geometrically patterned soundhole. I too have been fascinated by the delicacy that's achieved solely, in Bruce's case, with small chisels shaped from metal engraving tools.

I don't think I'm wrong in anticipating a question about how a rose is carved so before you ask, let me show you.

Bruce began lute making quite by accident. In 1974, when he was only sixteen, he was looking

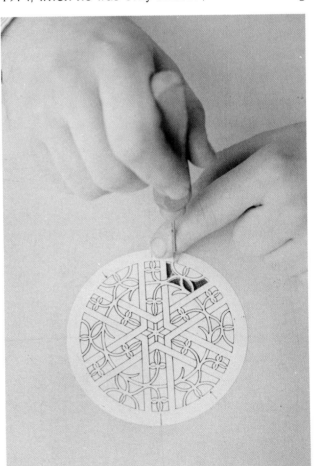

BRUCE DUNCAN

1

2

CARVING A LUTE ROSE

1 The design, on paper, is glued to the correct spot on the lute top.
2. With fine, sharp chisels Bruce cuts away the negative spaces of the design.

3. Ridges and contours are shaped with knives.
4. The completed rose.

3

4

for someone to teach him how to make a classical guitar but was instead sent to Michael Schreiner, a lute maker. Building lutes seemed equally interesting, so he stayed with it and, while still in high school, spent late afternoons, after class, with Michael.

As well as being an amateur musician dabbling in guitar, lute, flute, recorder and even synthesizer, woodworking had aways been a hobby with Bruce. These two separate pursuits, music and woodworking, are united in instrument making and that, surely, enhanced its attraction for him.

During the following six years, he spent his time between London, England and Toronto. Twice, for a total period of about a year, he was in the London shop of Stephen Gottlieb, the

eminent British luthier and teacher. There was also a return stretch of two years with Michael Schreiner in Toronto, helping Michael construct student lutes.

Although his grandfather and great-grandfather were both woodworkers, Bruce's family is still only starting to come round to the idea of their son's lute making profession. Since 1981, however, Bruce has been producing one lute per month and intends to do all he can to remain in lute making full time. He builds, on commission, any style of Renaissance or Baroque lute.

The lute's bowl is one of its more unique and striking features. It is traditionally constructed over a mould of the bowl's shape. The centre rib, already pre-bent, is aligned and attached to wooden blocks which will be the

Bruce Duncan demonstrating his method of glueing lute ribs together. He pins them in place, one rib at a time, over the mould until the bowl of the body is completely shaped.

strengthening reinforcements at opposite ends of the bowl. Then the next rib on either side of the centre one is bent, fitted and glued. This continues until all the ribs are attached to each other and the actual bowl shape is realized. The joints between these ribs are reinforced on the inside by strips of parchment or linen.

Unlike the guitars we've seen with their lacquer or polyurethene finish or the violin family of instruments which were finished with varnish, Bruce uses a finish of pulmerized turpentine.

Pulmerizing is a process of exposing the turpentine to ultraviolet sunlight while simultaneously impregnating it with oxygen. It is then cooked to darken it slightly. The duration of the cooking determines its colour. Bruce's finishing process is, for me, yet another addition to the already fascinating and controversial world of musical instrument finishing.

We have a true change of pace coming to us with the next instrument.

7 Steel Drums
Earle Wong

EARLE WONG

For this instrument, we leave the world of wood and gut behind. What began life as a 45-gallon oil drum made with eighteen gauge steel has been transformed into a tonally subtle, sweet-sounding musical instrument. This is a chromed soprano steel drum or steel pan, as it is more commonly called. Steel pans are built to encompass the entire musical spectrum normally found in an orchestra — soprano, alto, tenor, baritone and bass. Each set of pans, with either one, two, three or in the case of the bass, as many as twelve separate drums is tuned to the corresponding musical range. As an example, the lowest note of a paired set of soprano drums is middle C and the highest is the first E you'd encounter once you'd passed two octaves above middle C.

Earle Wong, a Trinidadian living in Toronto since 1968, built and tuned these pans. He completes most of his rough work in an old schoolhouse on Trinity Street that has become his workshop. The usual custom in steel drum circles of being both the band or orchestra leader and the maker/tuner of the band's instruments is alive and well in Toronto. Earle began Toronto's first steel band, The Steeltones, based at the Univeristy of Toronto and builds instruments for numerous other bands, school boards and individuals.

Immediately upon arrival in Toronto, Earle joined a bandleader friend whom he had performed with in Trinidad and began learning to make drums. He continued performing professionally and making drums until 1979, when his friend left Toronto, and Earle had no choice but to learn how to properly tune what he knew how to construct.

Builders of steel drums differentiate between those who build the drums and those who are able to properly fine tune the notes to produce the accurate harmonics. The latter are referred to as tuners. There is no quick route to becoming a skilled tuner. It is an ability that comes only from years of trial and error, watching other tuners and amassing information from wherever possible. Since the steel drum is still evolving as a legitimate serious instrument — it's only forty

years old — there is little documentation or instruction on how to hammer out the notes and tune accurately. In part to help rectify that, Earle, for years, has been working on a book about drum construction and steel bands.

GARY: Are all these little bumps the marks left by the 'hammering out'?

Right.

GARY: You mean, to bring the music out of the steel, they really use hammers?

Yes. That's all that's used.

But it's in the procedures that things get tricky.

Six, nine and twelve pound sledge-hammers are used in the early stages of sinking and stretching the metal cap to its prescribed length, the paper-thin dish, pushed to a depth of eight inches in this soprano pan, is then sectioned out. The areas for each note have been calculated in proportion to their pitch and are literally pounded up section by section with a two pound hammer. At this point, the drum is heated or *burned* to temper the steel before the fine tuning begins.

If I take this small steel dowel tipped in rubber and tap this note, an F, exactly in the middle section like so, we hear the basic note. If I tap the same section but nearer to the rim like so, we hear the F note but an octave higher. If I once again tap the same section but closer to its left edge, we hear a harmonic of the note, in this case a C. All of these different tonal responses are some of the reasons behind Earle's achievement of each note's clear full ring. Obtaining these and other harmonic subtleties is the job of a tuner.

GEORGES: What made people start using an oil drum for music?

Phew! That's a big question.

I imagine that because it came out of Trinidad's folk culture, there is no clear record of its beginning, but enough is known to make educated guesses. Most authorities agree that the Bamboo Tamboo was Trinidad's earliest percussive instrument. In an effort to improve on it through the years, other objects with stronger or more interesting sounds were sought. In this

The job left to contemporary builders like Earle is the refining and standardizing that has yet to happen to the steel pan as is has to most other acoustic instruments.

If any of you would like to have a try at playing this or any other instrument in the show — and I can see that some of you have been itching to do so — we'll be glad to set up an appointment for you after regular gallery hours. So please restrain yourselves during the tour — as difficult as I know that will be to do.

Our next stop returns us to the classical world with another maker's rendition of my favourite of the violin family.

DEBORAH: Which instrument is that?

See for yourself, it's here on your right....

century, metal cans, tins and some of the big oil drums were used sporadically. The big drums were first brought to the Island by the American Navy. After the Second World War, the quantity of empty oil drums around the naval base increased dramatically and led, naturally, to a greater amount of experimentation.

A slow process of attempting to produce different notes while using the drums primarily as rhythm instruments resulted in the crucial inspirations of three individuals that transformed the oil drum into a musical instrument. One person made the bowl concave, allowing space for more notes. Another devised the spider web pattern of notation, and a third began applying the science of acoustics to the tuning.

Earle Wong chromed soprano steel pan.

8 Cellos, Violas
Richard Kirstiuk

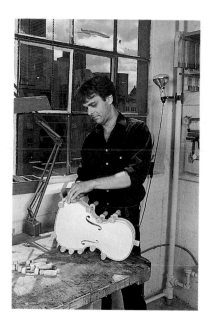

RICHARD KIRSTIUK

DEBORAH: This is a cello, isn't it?

That it is.

DEBORAH: Why is it your favourite?

Oh...for a couple of reasons. I'm attracted to the aesthetics inherent in all instruments of the violin family, but the cello's larger yet still approachable size is its appeal. For me, the cello is a work of sclupture, with its substantial curves and expanses of beautiful woods. Then there is its pitch. Tuned a full octave below a viola, which itself is tuned a fifth lower than a violin, it yields such resonant and rich, low sounds that I find it particularly seductive.

In the year 1572, Andrea Amati, working in Cremona Italy, made what has become one of the earliest known cellos. To all appearances, Amati's work was the prelude to the serious refining of the instrument throughout the following century by all of that time's known makers.

Richard Kirstiuk, has continued that tradition with this beautiful cello. At present, Richard prefers European curly maple for the bodies and necks and German silver spruce for the tops. Depending on the particular style of cello or viola he is making, the work takes him from six to twelve weeks to complete. Making a historical copy with the preparatory work and slower building that it entails requires far more time than an instrument of his own design.

SAMUEL: We've seen one other viola so far...

True, we have.

SAMUEL: Well, I'm assuming that each of these makers uses appropriate woods and knows how to construct properly his instruments....

True again.

SAMUEL: Then what makes one maker's instruments so different from another's?

Absolutely every part of an instrument affects its sound to some degree so when you change even one small dimension or thickness you affect the result. In truth, if you had two different makers building the same instrument using the same woods, methods, and dimensions, you would have two different sounding instruments with, at most, a few similar characteristics.

So, begin with two separate makers, each working with his or her own ideas as to shape, thicknesses and measurements for each and every part. Next, add the complication of different pieces of the same species of wood, each with distinguishing properties because of where it grew. For example, if it came from one particular side of a mountain, it might have received more rain than the other side thus producing wider spring growth, i.e., the space in between the grain lines, which in turn may mean more flexibility but less response to higher vibrations. That is just one small example.

We must also consider the 'free water' and 'bound water' contents of the wood's cell structure. The former, held in the cell's cavity, affects the expansion and contraction of the wood through the seasons and the latter, contained in the cell walls, affects the wood's strength and vibrating properties.

I could talk for hours on the subject of what causes one instrument to be different or better than the next. I assure you I won't but I think that with the few points I've mentioned, you get the picture.

MARTHA: 'Scuse me?

Yes?

MARTHA: Have these instruments always had the curly part at the top?

Do you mean the scroll?

MARTHA: I guess so.

Scroll shaped pegheads can be found on instruments from as early as the beginning of the 16th century. Since that takes us back to before the Amati cello I described, I think we can assume that the majority of cello pegheads and for that matter, those of violas and violins have been scrolls.

MICHAEL: How do you make the scrolls?

Well, I've never actually done one but I can tell you how a maker such as Richard does it.

It is carved and shaped from the solid neck piece. Once it is sawn to a rough approximate size, the work is done with gouge chisels, files and lastly, finished with scrapers and sandpaper. First to be shaped is the volute, the central core of the scroll. The fluting* on the perimeters of the head is done next. That is followed by the drilling out and chiseling smoothe of the inner peg-box.

Originally from Vancouver, Richard has been in Toronto since 1975. He was working for Ford of Canada as an apprentice electrician before he began making musical instruments. Constructing a classical guitar was his introduction to lutherie but the available help of two other makers lured him to the violin family.

The first was Jonathan Connover, a viola

1

3

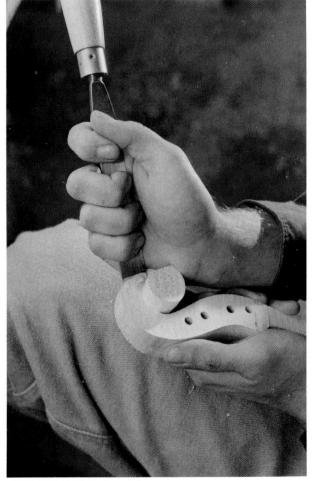

2

4

SHAPING OF THE SCROLL

1. Richard first pencils the outline of the neck shape onto a squared block of curly maple.
2. The rough shaping is cut on a bandsaw.
3. The taper of the neck up to the scroll is carefully sawn away. In the foreground are the cutoffs.
4. The volute or central core of the scroll is shaped with a gouge chisel.

*see glossary

5. The fluting on the perimeter of the scroll and head is cut with smaller gouges.
6. The inner peg-box is first drilled out then chiselled smooth.
7. Chiseling the delicate points of the scroll preceeds the final stage of smoothing all surfaces with scrapers and sandpaper.

5

6

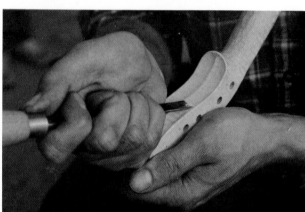

7

maker now working in the United States. It was Mr. Connover who attracted Richard to the woodworker's co-operative workshop that occupied the second floor of an aging John Street industrial building, until April 1984. It was in that Soho co-op that he received also the advice and assistance of the Ecuadorian craftsman Olivo Chiliquinga. For eight years, until 1985 when he returned to Ecuador Mr. Chiliquinga lived and worked in Toronto. While here, he gave freely to Richard and others of his accumulated expertise as a third generation luthier capable of building virtually any stringed musical instrument.

Since 1981, after having cautiously tested the waters for one year making cellos part-time, Richard has relied solely on his cello, viola and occasionally violin making for his living. His first customers were music students but symphony musicians rapidly replaced them. Many have ordered copies of their own time worn, but beloved, cellos. Richard's shop space, shared with Mr. Chiliquinga until the latter's move south, until very recently remained a component of the re-located co-op.

It might be the fact that he too plays the cello a bit or it might simply be a typical trait of a devoted instrument maker that Richard's most gratifying moment in the building process is when he places his instrument in able hands and hears it played. It is those moments that remind builders and players of the most challenging and most rewarding aspect of musical instrument making — instilling in an object made of wood, metal, porcelain, ivory, glass or whatever, the ability to produce stirring musical sounds!

Are there any questions? Yes....?

DOUG: So like how come a cello's called a cello?

Well, about all I can tell you is that it began life with the name violoncino, meaning small violon. By the late 1600s when the instrument, used for the bass part of a violin orchestra, had been made smaller, more elegant and more portable, it came to be called the violoncello. That smaller size corresponds approximately to the dimensions of a modern cello and I imagine the prefix violon has just dropped out of usage through the centuries. The full word, violoncello, is still the correct name.

If we're all set then, it is time to view the work of Matthew Redsell.

9 Harpsicords, Virginals
Matthew Redsell

Standing here in all their majesty are both a single-manual and a double-manual harpsichord, named for the number of keyboards they employ. Matthew Redsell is their maker yet, according to Matthew, the single-manual is but his version of an instrument built in the early 17th century in Antwerp, Belgium by the Ruckers family. The double-manual is his reproduction of an 18th century instrument built by Daniel Dulcken, also of Antwerp.

For more than 150 years, the harpsichord and its music were all but forgotten, overshadowed by newer instruments and musical trends. It wasn't until the turn of this century that a resurgence of interest in the harpsichord flowered into an international movement of builders and players. The strong fascination for the instrument, its music and its times has remained and strengthened in our contemporary music world.

Builders such as Matthew Redsell incorporate their own improvements and modifications into the construction of their instruments while staying faithful to the designs of the original master builders. So, although Matthew may refer to one of these as a Dulcken copy, his own innovations are hidden underneath the soundboard or in his methods of construction.

A Redsell harpsichord is composed of these basic parts: the case, sides and lid made from basswood, but the steam bent side is poplar; the soundboard is Sitka spruce; the pin block which anchors the pins near the keyboard to which the strings are attached is maple; the narrow curved bridges sitting on the soundboard are made of beech; the keyboard's naturals* are either made entirely of bone or walnut; the sharps are ebony; the jacks, into which are mounted the bird quill or delrin plastic that actually plucks the string, are made of basswood along with all the other parts of the *key assemblies*.

The keyboard and action or, collectively, the key assembly as Matthew calls it, is the most complex and crucial segment of the instrument. Most of its complicated workings are hidden from view. If we could see behind the nameboard or the front piece of the frame, we'd see how the extensions of the keys, resting on balance pins, connect with the jacks which pluck the strings on their rise and dampen the strings on their return.

Matthew's interest in the keyboard began as a player. He came to Toronto in 1971 to attend the University of Toronto's music faculty. Five years of studying piano and composition gave him his general music degree but not the satisfaction he needed. "A conscious evaluation of my abilities had turned me to instrument building." He taught himself how to build harpsichords in a basement during his spare time throughout these university years. His first, built in 1973, was from an acquired set of plans. His second, completed two years later, coincided with the completion of his music studies and helped him make the decision to build full time.

To teach himself the methods of harpsichord construction, Matthew travelled to the shops of other makers, but as with most self-taught craftspeople, he learned the most from his own mistakes. He feels that it was only in 1983, after eight years of full-time work, that his instruments finally reached the top-notch level of quality that he has since maintained. With the help of one full-time and two part-time cabinet-makers, he is now able to complete two or three double-manual harpsichords and six virginals every year.

LINDA: Why is there wallpaper over some parts. Is this a cheap model or something?

Shhh. . . . It's a good thing Matthew's not around to hear you say that: He might take offense!

I realize though, it is not household knowledge that many harpsichords traditionally had some parts of their cases covered in papers. Those that Matthew has used are from hand cut, specially printed sheets. In combination with the gold leaf and gold banding, they connote a better quality instrument, not a cheaper one.

GARY: I heard the term choir used with harpsichords but I never found out what it meant.

The term itself is easy to explain. If you'll just peer under the lid of the double-manual

MATTHEW REDSELL

Matthew Redsell single manual harpsichord. Case: basswood and poplar; soundboard: spruce; keyboard: ebony, cherry, beech; music stand and pin cover: cherry; gold leaf; printed papers. 226cm. x 92cm.

you'll see three different layers of strings. Each layer or set is called a choir. So on this instrument there are three choirs. Two are referred to as eight-foot choirs, not because they are eight-foot long but because they correspond in pitch to eight-foot long pipe of an organ. The third is named the four-foot choir because its strings are half as long as the eight-foot and hence its notes are an octave higher.

When the keys of the lower manual are pressed, they connect with jacks that pluck all three choirs. However, the keys of the upper manual, by a similar action, pluck only one of the eight-foot choirs but can do it in two different spots.

Another question?

GARY: Have you forgotten the virginal?

Oh! Good for you. I almost did.

Virginals are members of the harpsichord family with similar kinds of constructions but are smaller, obviously, and are essentially simpler instruments.

Matthew's has a pine case, Sitka spruce soundboard, cherry mouldings*, an oak pinblock, basswood bottom and inside framing, and its keyboard has cherry naturals with the ebony sharps. I could describe other differences between Matthew's two keyboard instruments, but you should be able to spot many of them yourself. So, to allow you the chance to do that, let's remain here an extra few minutes.

*see glossary

While Matthew Redsell's work is fresh in your eye and mind, I want to mention a fact about him that I saved until now, In whatever spare time he can accumulate, Matthew publishes a magazine called *Continuo, An Early Music Magazine*. Early music refers to music from the Renaissance and Baroque periods of western history, i.e. from the late 14th century to the middle of the 18th. The harpsichord family of instruments and its music fall within early music's boundaries, hence Matthew's commitment.

I've brought up the early music label at this moment for your fuller understanding of why the particular instruments you're about to see come next.

Before us are two instruments that are inseparable from early music. Philip Davis, their maker, calls them viols. The Italians call them violas da gamba, while to the Germans, they are known as gambas. To musical historians they are valued by whatever name for what they truly are — the last significant stage in the evolution of the bowed guitar family

The smaller of the two is a lyra bass, the larger a full bass. Both are built with European curly maple for the back, sides and neck; German spruce for the top; ebony or curly maple for the fingerboard; ebony again for the tailpiece and tuning pegs.

At first glance, these instruments may seem similar to cellos and their like, but they are very different. Most apparent is the different body shape and the soundholes in the shape of 'C'

holes rather than 'F' holes. Next, but still as obvious, is the increased number of strings. Our lyra bass has six, and the bass has seven, its common maximum number. The necks each have seven gut frets tied and knotted as on a lute neck. The tops have been arched by carving from a solid piece of wood as in the violin family, but the arch is absolutely convex from neck to end-block, making it very strong and very different from a violin or cello.

The backs are more unusual. They are perfectly flat for the most part but with a characteristic kink about five-sixths of the way up. From that ridge, the back slants towards the neck at a relatively steep angle. I'll turn this bass viol around and you'll see what I'm describing.

Ahh... I thought you'd react like that. The inlay and carving work on this instrument is truly impressive. Philip achieved these intricate geometric patterns by painstakingly inlaying wooden strips of purfling. In that decoration alone are dozens of work hours. Coupled with the time spent in carving the relief patterns on the back and sculpting the peghead, it is apparent we are viewing a labour of love by a talented artisan.

Philip had been playing guitar through the 1960s and had already put in three years of study in the wood shop of the Ontario College of Art when he decided to build a classical guitar with the help of a book and his teacher's moral support. "When I started the guitar project, it was 1972 and I was twenty-three, it was for me, then, bringing all the threads of my interests together."

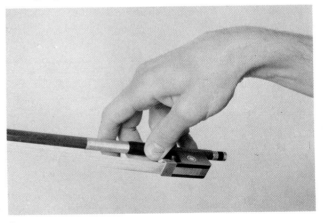

PHILIP DAVIS

1. Philip demonstrates the proper hand position for a baroque bass viol bow on one of is own making.
2. Philip demonstrates the comparative hand position on a modern cello bow.

1

2

Once bitten by the instrument-making bug, he succumbed to its powers.

After leaving O.C.A., he worked in Quebec City, first as a cabinetmaker and then as a draftsman. He found time to build a few instruments in between his day work, but the "love of working wood — the scale of that work, the care it demands and a deepening interest in music" pulled him away from Quebec and over to London, England. The London College of Furniture has the most thorough musical instrument courses in the English-speaking world, with instruction in the theories and techniques of construction keyboard, bowed, fretted or woodwind instruments. Philip spent three years at the college studying early fretted instruments and bows.

On his return to Quebec City, he set up shop in his apartment for a further three years, then Toronto beckoned. "I came back to Toronto to be among more makers, more suppliers and a wider range of musicians than in Quebec City." In his first year here, he established the instrument building workshop at O.C.A. which has since expanded to a year-round program.

Between the summers of 1983 and 1984, our mobile Mr. Davis was back in Europe for specialized learning. With the help of a classically trained violin and viol maker, Jurgen J. Schroder of Frankfurt, Germany, and with his own travels to instrument collections in Brussels and Paris, Philip accumulated a wealth of that specialized knowledge. He is and will continue to apply that valuable experience to his instrument building and especially to restoration, the more demanding work. Most important to us is that he is doing it all here in Toronto.

SAMUEL: I was curious whether one could use a cello bow on a viol?

Well, if a cello bow was all you had, I suspect you could make do, but a baroque bow is very different. Instead of the more familiar pernambuco and ebony, it is made from snakewood and has an ivory frog. There is also less camber or curve in the wood of the baroque bow. Where it's most unique, however, is in the way it's held. Unlike the violin or cello bow, the frog is grasped from underneath, thus bringing different pressures and movements into the playing. It is no coincidence that Philip makes baroque bows as well as the viols.

11 Classical and Steel String Guitars
William Laskin

I have some difficulty with these next instruments! I too am an instrument maker, as you must have understood by now, and since my workshop is in Toronto I really had to be included in this show. My difficulty is how to chat about myself without either getting carried away or being so afraid I might blow my own horn louder than any of the others that I understate myself.

DEBORAH: Oh, come on, don't be shy! We want to hear about you.

Well...I guess I should tell you some things about myself but please, stop me if I go overboard.

As you can see by these two instruments, I am a guitar maker. I devote equal time to both steel string, classical, and flamenco guitars but manage to produce a hybrid tenor mandolin once or twice a year.......It's so hard to decide

where to begin when the topic is yourself.

DEBORAH: Why don't we ask you some questions to get you going?

How come there's a part missing from the body of that guitar?

That's called a *cutaway*. We've seen it on one other acoustic guitar so far, as well as on the electrics. The body of my steel guitar is cut away on that side simply to make it easier to play the higher frets.

JOHN: Do you play guitar?

Yes. I've been playing since I was nine years old. I play a number of stringed instruments and some stranger instruments as well: the English bagpipes and the concertina.

MICHAEL: Tell us how you became a guitar maker.

Thank you. I was waiting for someone to ask me that. Permit me to begin at the beginning.

I'm from Hamilton, a city sixty kilometers from here, and I came to Toronto to work in a recording studio when I was seventeen. At the time, sound studio engineering was what I thought I wanted to do. But six months of being overworked and having to deal with the business side of music changed my mind. As I was contemplating quitting and living off performing music, I met the guitar maker Jean Larrivée at a Mariposa Folk Festival and an earlier idea took shape. At first, it was only a vague and naive plan of mine to travel someday to the west coast and apprentice myself to a guitar maker I'd heard about. But once I met Jean, a friendly talented craftsman, and he agreed to take me on, my decision to quit work was made.

So in the fall of 1971, having just turned eighteen, I began the two most delightful years of my teenage life. For the majority of those two years I worked alone with Jean seven days a week from 10:30 in the morning until midnight. It was exciting being so young with no responsibilities and almost no living expenses and able to totally immerse myself in guitar making. And Jean was an excellent, understanding teacher.

After six months, I'd built my first guitar and by the second year, I was responsible for close to

WILLIAM LASKIN

William Laskin steel string cutaway guitar. German spruce, E.Indian rosewood, mahogany, ebony. Body : 51.3cm. x 40.5cm.

half the work on each of Jean's instruments.

In the fall of 1973, I set up my own shop in a basement and was ready to produce. I recall having a half dozen orders for instruments before I owned even a saw. I knew I was benefitting from the reputation of my teacher. After one year, I separated shop and home, and now, three different shops and more than fifteen years later, here I am. I still spend six days a week in the shop working with an unending drive to build the finest guitar in the world. That challenge, truly, is what it's all about!

Didn't I tell you I would go on and on if you neglected to stop me? I ought to begin discussing these guitars of mine....

DEBORAH: Wait. Let us or me, at least, take a guess at which woods you've used.

Ok, let's see how well you do.

DEBORAH: The bodies are rosewood?

Right.

DEBORAH: The neck of one is mahogany but the other I don't know.

You're right about the steel string neck but on my classical guitars I use curly maple. Its weight and density add among other things noticeable sustain to the notes. Do you want to keep going?

DEBORAH: Yup. I can tell that the fingerboards are ebony and the tops are....spruce.

You almost had a perfect score. The steel string's top is spruce, but the top on this classical is western red cedar from British Columbia. I'm impressed though. You folks must actually be listening to me. Another question?

SAMUEL: Could you tell us about the work on the head of the cutaway guitar? I've never seen anything like that on an instrument before.

You have just broached one of my pet subjects. Inlay. Inlay work on musical instruments has been a tradition since before the Renaissance. Most contemporary inlays are based on simpler representational depictions of such objects as potted flowers, dragons or an occasional semiclad woman. Some of the other guitar

1

2

3

4

INLAYING

1. I draw out the peghead figure completely on paper.
2. I glue the outlined patterns of each separate part to their respective materials, (in this photo it's a part of the dancer's dress), and cut them carefully with a fret saw.
3. I assemble and glue together the various pieces of the inlay, almost like a jig-saw puzzle, and scribe its position onto the peghead.
4. I cut a cavity into the ebony with a tiny router.

40

makers in this show have surpassed the norm with their inlays, but I seem to have stumbled on a unique approach to design and an engraving style that draws more from illustration art than musical instrument traditions.

To depict most accurately this dancer I used mother-of-pearl shell, abalone shell, ivory, sterling silver and various burled wood veneers. I use whatever materials are necessary be they woods, precious metals, shells, or other natural substances to reproduce as accurately as possible the inherent colours and shades of the subject I am inlaying.

The black detailing lines such as those depicting her facial features are actually engraved cuts into the mother-of-pearl that are filled in with a type of wax.

Briefly then, this is how I do an inlay:....

MARTHA: Did you ever have to inlay anything really weird?

Luckily, no. I've certainly had some strange requests, but I refuse anything that I find distasteful.

One fellow wanted worm shapes inlaid into the pegboard! Another wanted a bird on the peghead in the process of dropping some you-know-what. His complete vision was to have lumps of this bird's droppings inlaid at random on the fingerboard with a big accumulated heap of the stuff at the last fret. These days, with most of my customers being professional musicians or dedicated amateurs, I'm either given orders for inlay designs that are appealing and challenging or often allowed free reign to do as I wish.

Inlay is an added creative dimension to musical instrument building that makes it, for me, all the more satisfying.

Now that you've seen a cross-section of the variety of instruments Toronto's makers produce, it's time to enter the larger second gallery.

5

7

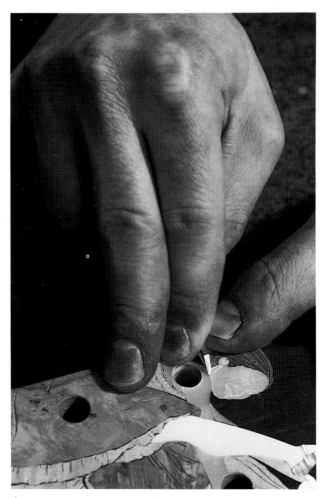

6

5. I epoxy and clamp the inlay into place.
6. Once sanded flush, I cut detail lines into the materials with a metal graver. You can see its cutting tip poking out from between a thumb and first finger.
7. Wiping off the rubbed-in engraver's wax reveals the defined graver's cuts.

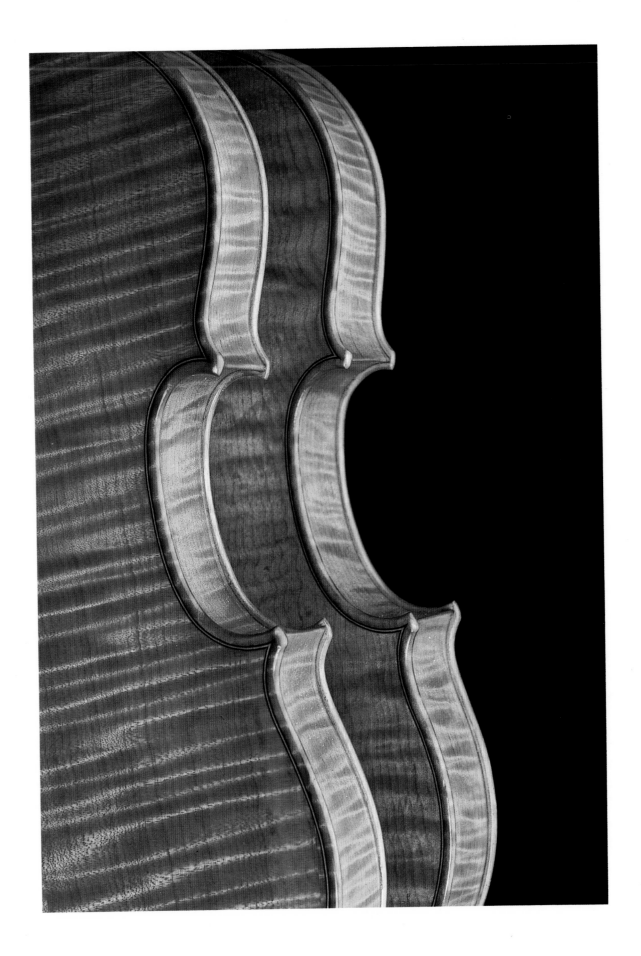

GREGORY WALKE

Gregory Walke violins. Detail of backs clearly showing curl figure in the maple.

43

Gregory Walke at work in West
Germany during a recent stint in
the workshop of luthier Michael
Franke.

2 Gregory Walke violin 59.5cm. x
20.5cm. and viola 69.5cm x 24.2cm.
both curly maple, spruce and
ebony.

1

2

1

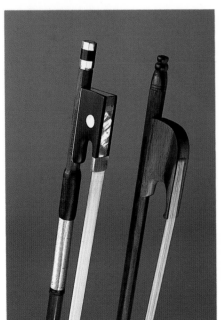

2

3

BARNARD WALKE

1 Bernard at his bench inspecting curve of 'stick' he is scraping to shape.

2 Bernard Walke bows. Detail of two frogs. Top: violin, pernambuco, ebony, mother of pearl, silver. Bottom: tenor viol, snakewood.

3 Bernard Walke bows. From top to bottom: bass viol 71.3cm., tenor viol 70.2cm., both of snakewood and horsehair; violin 74.2cm., cello 70.8cm. both of pernambuco, ebony, mother of pearl, silver and horsehair.

45

1

JACK AND MARA GOOSMAN

1 Goosman flute, solid gold, separated into its three joints. Assembled length 67cm.

2 The Goosman workshop. Yutaka Chiba (who, as this book went to press, left the Goosmans to establish his own flute repair shop) sights along the edge of a silver centre joint.

3 Silver tubing, partially completed flutes and templates for fingerhole placement from the Goosman workshop.

2

3

TWELVTH FRET

1 Twelvth Fret custom built double neck electric bass made from walnut, maple and Macassar ebony with EMG. electronics. 131.5cm. x 34.5cm.

2 Grant Macneill and Dan Charman in the storefront of their shop examining the fire engine red 'Fender copy' they built as a custom order.

3 Twelvth Fret solid body electric guitar. Their newest model. Made with mahogany, walnut, ebony, Gibson PAF and vintage Seymour Duncan Firebird pickups. 98cm. x 35cm. The body is thinned and shaped more than usual to reduce mass while the ebony pickguard helps to reduce static in studio situations. A roughed out blank of the same model sits behind.

1

2

3

SERGEI DE JONGE

1 Sergei De Jonge 17-string guitar. Detail of rear of mahogany neck/peghead.

1

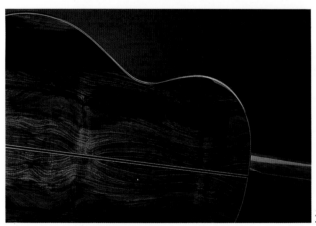

2 Sergei De Jonge 6-string classical guitar. Detail of Brazillian rosewood back.

3 Sergei in his shop stringing a new guitar.

3

1

2

3

DAVID WREN

1 David Wren in his workshop playing one of his sunburst stained steel string guitars.

2 David Wren steel string guitar. Detail showing innovative bridge design and abalone shell sound-hole inlay.

3 David Wren guitar. Detail of engraved peghead inlay on sunburst guitar. Brass, copper, stainless steel, mother of pearl, abalone shell, purpleheart wood.

49

BRUCE DUNCAN

1 Bruce Duncan; two lutes. Facing is a 7-course, mid to late 16th century type made with hard curly maple for the bowl, Swiss pine, beech and ebony; string length 58.3cm. Behind it is a 10-course, early 17th century type made with sycamore, pine, walnut and ebony; string length 63.5cm.

2 Bruce Duncan at his workbench lubricating his rib glueing mould.

1   2

2

EARLE WONG

1 Earle Wong taking a break from sinking the cap of a 45 gallon oil drum with sledge hammer.

2 Earle Wong chromed soprano steel pan.

51

1

RICHARD KIRSTIUK

1 Richard Kirstiuk in his workshop
assembling a viola body.

2 Richard Kirstiuk viola. European
curly maple, German spruce,
ebony. Full body length 68.9cm.

2

Richard Kirstiuk cello. European
curly maple, German silver spruce,
ebony 122.5cm. x 42.4cm.

1

MATTHEW REDSELL

1 Matthew Redsell double manual harpsichord. Case: basswood and poplar; soundboard: spruce; keyboard: ebony, bone, beech; music stand, pin cover: cherry; gold leaf; printed papers. 265cm. x 98cm.

2 Matthew Redsell, left, with employee Al Hughes examining the pins on a virginal. The case is pine and basswood, the soundboard spruce, the keyboard cherry and ebony. 150cm. x 50cm.

3 Sunlight bathes these Matthew Redsell keyboards of cherry and ebony on basswood; mounted on their poplar frames. The red felt located at the ends of the key extensions is the point on which the jacks rest.

2

3

54

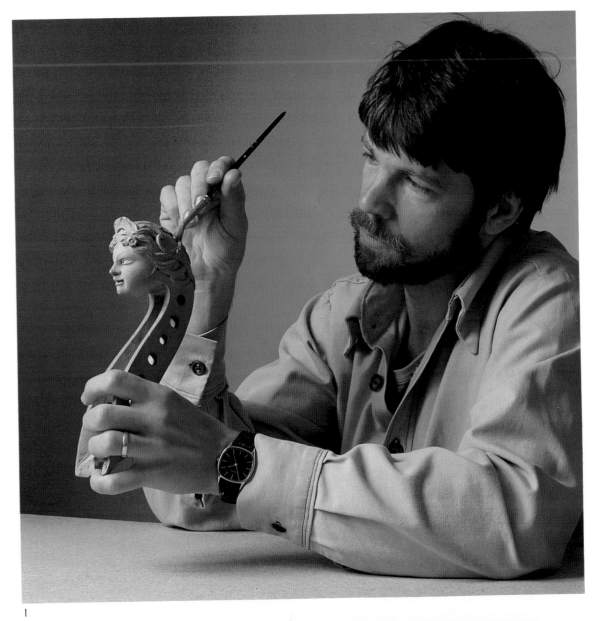

1

2

3

4

PHILIP DAVIS

1 Philip Davis restoring the head-stock of a Bertrand viol made in Paris in 1713.

2 Philip Davis lyra bass viol. Detail of lion's head carving of peg-box. 20.5cm. x 5cm.

3 Philip Davis bass viol. Detail of European curly maple back showing carving and wood strip inlaywork.

4 Philip Davis lyra bass viol. European curly maple, German spruce, ebony. 104.5cm. x 32.5cm.

WILLIAM LASKIN

1 William Laskin in his workshop.

2 William Laskin classical guitar.
Detail of curly maple neck and
upper back.

2

1

2

1 William Laskin steel string guitar peghead. Engraved inlay of mother of pearl, ivory, abalone shell, silver, various burled wood veneers. 17.3cm. x 7.1cm.

2 William Laskin classical guitar. Canadian Western Red Cedar, E.Indian rosewood, ebony, Canadian curly maple. Body: 49.5cm. x 37cm.

57

JOHN NEWTON

1 John Newton violin. Canadian
curly maple, Georgia pine, ebony.
58.5cm. x 20.8cm.

2 John Newton in his workshop.

3 John Newton viola. Canadian
curly maple, Georgia pine, ebony.
68.3cm. x 24.6cm.

1

2

3

1

2

PETER SHOEBRIDGE

1 Peter Shoebridge playing one of his porcelain flutes in his studio.

2 A stack of flute bodies recently glaze fired in the kiln.

59

JAMES FRIESON

James Frieson working at his bench on a soundhole rosette marquetry.

1

2

2 James Frieson flamenco guitar peghead showing marquetry work. 18cm. x 7.3cm. One of his hand polishing rags is in the background.

3 James Frieson marquetry guitar in process. Detail of back showing curly maple base wood to which will be glued the macassar ebony — itself inset with ivory, abalone shell, mother of pearl and numerous exotic wood veneers.

3

60

RAAD

Raad violin. Spruce top, ebony fingerboard, maple neck. 61.3 cm x 17.5 cm.

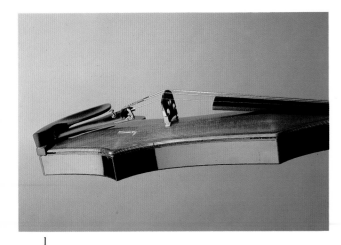

1

1 Raad violin. Detail showing
"floating top" suspended on
dense foam at points of the bouts
and soft, breathable fill-in foam in
between.

2 Richard Armin, Jim Jones and
Jonathan Borah (top) of Raad
instruments in one of their electronics studios with one of their
electric cellos; 127cm. x 36.8cm.
Fibre composite back, spruce top,
ebony fingerboard, maple neck.
Jim is using an electronic probe to
investigate responses on the top
plate.

2

MONTI EGAN

1 Monti Egan playing one of his celtic harps. This one is built of oak with a cedar soundboard.

2 Monti Egan classical guitar. Back view showing E. Indian rosewood back and sides, mahogany neck. Body: 49.5cm. x 36.2cm.

PETER NOY

1 Peter Noy Irish flute and alto
recorder both of boxwood and
imitation ivory. The flute's key is
silver. Both instruments rest on a
tiny log of boxwood.

2 Peter Noy in his workshop examining the curly maple mouthpiece section of a tenor recorder.

64

1

KOLYA PANHUYSEN

1 Kolya Panhuysen guitar. Brazillian rosewood back and sides,
Canadian red cedar top, ebony
fingerboard, mahogany neck.
100cm. x 36.6cm.

2 Kolya Panhuysen at his workbench shaping the slots in a classical guitar peghead.

2

65

MICHAEL SCHREINER

1 Michael Shreiner in his studio
holding his chitarrone. The bowl
and neck are Yew, the top is German spruce, the fingerboard is
ebony. 140cm. x 37.5cm.

2 Michael Schreiner chitarrone.
Detail of rose.

2

Michael Schreiner. Five lute bowls variously of yew and curly sycamore. Visible on the one upright is the paper taping that reinforces the rib joints.

1

2

1 Linda Manzer. Detail of customized instrument Linda dubbed Pikasso. It contains one conventional 6-string steel string guitar, a short scale fretless 12-string guitar plus two separate additional sets of 12 strings: one tuned to a chord and available for strumming, the other existing to sympathetically pick up and enhance vibrations from the other strings.

2 Linda Manzer archtop guitar. Curly maple back, sides and neck, German spruce top, ebony fingerboard, bridge and tailpiece. Body:51cm. x 42cm. This sunburst finish and all other lacquering of Linda's instruments is done by George Gray. He has a shop just outside of Toronto where he does finish work on musical instruments and furniture and occasionally finds time to build a few guitars of his own.

3 Linda Manzer in her shop working on her near-completed steel string cutaway guitar.

1

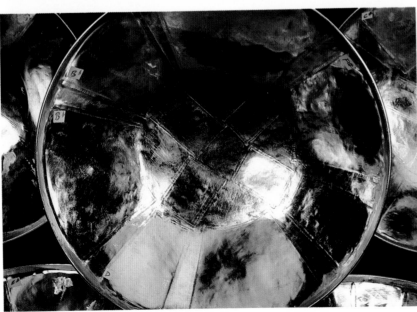

2

STEELTONE

1 Ed Peters, left, and Michael Salvatore or Steeltone sitting amidst a forest of their brass plated steel pans.

2 Steeltone pan 54cm. across. Detail of one of four tenor pans offering the visible evidence of Ed's and Michael's original approach to delineating the note areas. Note the squared off bottom curves of the normally rounded U shapes.

69

ROBIN GREEN

1 Robin Green classical guitar. E.
Indian rosewood, German spruce,
mahogany, ebony. 101cm. x 37.5
cm.

2 Robin Green at his workbench.
A partially completed guitar body
sits to his left.

70

ANASTAS FOTEV

1 Anastas Fotev viola. Detail of body. Yugoslavian curly maple back and sides, German spruce top. Full body length: 42cm.

2 Anastas Fotev at work on a viola.

1

2

JOE LADO

1 Joe Lado solid body electric guitars. The coloured, lacquered and airbrushed bodies are made from zebrawood, padauk or bird's-eye maple. The necks are a laminate of maple/padauk or rosewood/maple.

2 Joe Lado in his workshop holding an unfinished electric bass guitar. Note the laminated through-the-body neck construction.

1

2

1

2

CONSTANTIN TINGAS

1 Constantin Tingas lining the interior of a bouzouki.

2 Constantin Tingas bouzouki 96.5cm. x 29cm. and classical guitar 101cm. x 37.3cm. The bouzouki has a walnut bowl and spruce top. Surrounding the soundhole are inlaid plastics. The guitar has E. Indian rosewood, spruce, mahogany and ebony.

73

MASA-TOSHI INOKUCHI

1 Masa-toshi Inokuchi violin. Canadian curly maple back, sides and neck. Sitka spruce top. 58.7cm. x 21cm.

2 Masa-toshi Inokuchi holding an unfinished violin and a large piece of the Ontario curly maple that he located and cut himself. He is seated at the counter of the family's restaurant, the complete furnished interior of which he built.

1

2

74

SECOND GALLERY

12 Violas, Violins
John Newton

"A natural transition from the model airplanes of childhood" is how the articulate John Newton, maker of this violin and viola, rationalizes his entry into the luthier's trade. Like many instrument makers, John chose to make instruments because he couldn't afford to buy his desired instrument. And once his brother successfully built a violin with only the help of a book, John was intrigued and followed suit.

Undaunted by having failed his high school shop class, John completed his own first violin in 1975 and, like his brother, with only a book for guidance. John had finished four additional violins on his own when he met the world-renowed viola and violin maker, Otto Erdesz.

Hungarian-born, Mr. Erdesz came to Canada after a seventeen year residency in New York City,

where he earned the title of viola king. Although Mr. Erdesz has, unfortunately for us, recently returned to New York after eight years in Toronto, it was while working here that he saw John's self-taught efforts and was impressed enough to offer to teach him. John's apprenticeship began and continued for a couple of months as a full-time pursuit. Then for the following two years, from 1979 to 1981, John was in Mr. Erdesz's shop "on and off from one week to the next."

Summing up his learning experience with Mr. Erdesz, John remarked: "From Otto I learned so much about the ways to produce an excellent sounding instrument". John went on to explain that "the sound of a violin is so complex — it's not just the result of doing this and this and this like some scientific analysis purports".

Although many violin makers believe it necessary, John has found no need for specific tuning of the top and back plates.

LOUISE: Excuse me, What do you mean by tuning the top and back?

That refers to a maker's conscious effort to have the finished top and back vibrate at specified tones.

If you held a finished violin top or back at the correct spot and tapped it with your other hand, it would vibrate and ring freely. That ring is known as the principal plate tone or as it is more often labelled by makers, the tap tone. Many violin makers believe that there should be a separation of from a semitone* to a tone* between the principal plate tones of the top and back. The desired tone is achieved by controlled carving and final thicknessing* of the plates. Each and every section of the top and back affects the resulting sound and vibrational responses of the instrument. In an effort to deduce a thicknessing configuration for a given piece of wood, some makers use controlled frequency tuning of specific areas of the top and back, others use tap tones, still others flex the wood in various ways with their hands, which allows them to assess its characteristics by experienced feel. Clearly, John is in the latter categories.

JOHN NEWTON

John Newton viola. Canadian curly maple, Georgia pine, ebony. 68.3cm. x 24.6cm.

On this violin and viola, John has used primarily Canadian woods: curly maple for the bodies, and for the top a spruce that is similar to douglas fir which his teacher refers to as Georgia pine. John enjoys working with native woods and has proven to his own satisfaction that they result in superb instruments. The Georgia pine top specifically contributes to a mellower, older sound.

In the few years since John began building professionally, his production of one instrument per month has been enough to bring him to the attention of symphony and philharmonic orchestra musicians. That is an impressive feat in the competitive world of violin making, a world where some of his rival luthiers have been dead for more than 100 years!

The nature of violin construction and design is such that, if properly cared for, the instrument can withstand the tensions of being strung and played for centuries. Musicians have the advantage of being able to purchase well played in instruments and frequently ignore contemporary makes. Some players believe that newer instruments are not as good as old ones. Others have no patience to wait for a new instrument's own played in sound to develop.

In spite of these views, and like many other current violin makers, John feels he "would'nt be doing this if [he] didn't think it was possible to make an excellent NEW instrument". I, of course, am in full agreement with him.

Let's move slightly to the adjacent display for another of my abrupt changes. Once again we'll leave wood behind. This time for a substance uncommon to western musical instruments....

13 Porcelain Flutes
Peter Shoebridge

Before us are three slip-casted flutes, formed using a high fired, white ceramic clay: porcelain.
MICHAEL: How does one slip-cast a flute?

Whoa! You're a step ahead of me. I was going to tell you exactly that.

Peter Shoebridge, a professional potter, is the maker of these flutes. In 1983, for example, he made approximately 250 in one long process with the aid of two assistants.

Slip-casting is essentially a moulding procedure. Beginning with a soup mixture of eighty percent clay and twenty percent water, the chemical sodium silicate is added to separate electrostatically the bits of clay into a muddy consistency. This muddy soup, or the slip, is poured into plaster moulds. The plaster absorbs the water in the mixture, allowing the clay to dry against the mould's inner walls. The resulting dried cast *green* ware is then supported on wooden rods while the finger holes are drilled. Finally, as with most pottery, the flutes receive a bisque* firing in the kiln to harden the clay, then a second firing to fuse the overlaid glaze to the procelain.

Another instrument maker, Peter Noy, a maker of wooden flutes and recorders whose work we'll see later, assisted him in making the precisely tapered mandril* from which the moulds were made and in calculating the finger-hole spacing for the different models.

Yes?
MICHAEL: When the porcelain dries in the mould, doesn't it shrink?

As a matter of fact it does.

PETER SHOEBRIDGE

1

2

1. Helper Nguyen Trang at the vat where the soup mixture of clay, water and sodium silicate is stirred to a muddy consistency.
2. The plaster moulds into which the "slip" or soup mixture is poured.

*see glossary

79

Peter Shoebridge; three porcelain flutes. Top to bottom: Irish D flute 60cm. full length, Irish F flute 52cm. full length, baroque flute 60cm. full length.

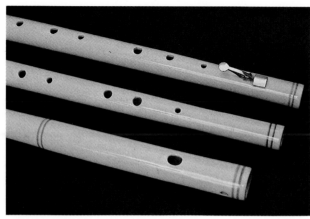

MICHAEL: Well, if the dimensions of the taper are important for the accuracy of the musical scale....

They are.

MICHAEL: .... how does Peter maintain that accuracy?

A perceptive question that is easy to answer.

The mandril's precise taper that I just spoke of has been accurately gauged to take into account the ten to twelve percent shrinkage of the clay. It's as simple as that.

The flute with the sterling silver key covering an additional hole is Peter's baroque model. The others, most often used for dance tunes, such as jigs, reels, waltzes, hornpipes, etc., is Peter's Irish models. Both uses for the porcelain flute jibe with its origins.

According to Peter, "porcelain was used for flutes in the baroque era and a few have survived in museums and private collections. The porcelain flute I build is adapted from a baroque flute of wood from about 1800, which itself was simplified for playing Irish folk music."

Born in England in 1949 but living in Toronto since he was about two years old, Peter had been playing classical guitar when he was impressed by concert (silver) flutists and their instruments. Soon after, he met Peter Noy who inspired him to make the porcelain flutes.

DOUG: Um.... say ya had one a' them flutes and ya didn't like it or somethin'. Could this guy just melt it down and make ya another? Y'know, just drop it back inta that soup or somethin'?

Ah.... not really. Once the clay and glaze have been fired, their compositions have been altered. They cannot be melted down.

I'ts one of the porcelain flute's appeals, actually, that it is unaffected by the temperatures and humidity levels that are the bane of wooden instruments.

Our next stop, neighbouring Peter Shoebridge's work, presents us with another novel approach to instrument making...

14 Flamenco Guitars, Marquetry Guitars
Jim Frieson

Although it may appear to you that these are just two more guitars, do not be deceived. Each, in its own way, is unique. One, a flamenco, is the only guitar like it in the show. Its companion, a three-quarter sized, ornately embellished, marquetry guitar is a rarity in all of contemporary instrument making.

Their maker, Jim Frieson, perfers to make flamenco guitars above all others, yet he spent more than a year constructing this other one-of-a-kind instrument. Occupying much of his spare time, it was a project to satisfy a personal fascination with marquetry techniques for musical instruments.

In the world's great instrument collections there exist some of the most elaborately decorated guitars ever built. The complexity of marquetry work on the fretted instrument family reached a peak in the late 17th century with the Hamburg (Germany) school of makers. The most famous of them was Joachim Tielke. His instruments, often built for royalty, were covered almost entirely with floral motifs and pictorial panels. The decorations were made by the application, carving and engraving of tortoise shell, ivory, pewter, mother-of-pearl and ebony.

In general, instrument makers after Tielke, primarily from the 18th century onward, sustained and nurtured a growing appreciation of unadorned workmanship. The quality and natural patterns of the woods, the overall proportions and the presence of accurate, clean hand work became the valued attributes. With the exception of the styles of ornamentation you've seen so far in the show, those criteria have remained the standards for appraising modern instruments. For that reason, Jim's marquetry endeavours are all the more unusual.

His geometrical designs and cartouches of flowers have been constructed from ivory, abalone, mother-of-pearl, ebony and numerous exotic wood veneers. On the body, the materials were attached with heated animal glues to a base of either curly maple or curly satinwood. Beneath the neck overlays is a base of poplar (or mahogany).

The flamenco guitar has a very different but no less distinctive history. Flamenco is the musical tradition of southern Spain. It has united dance, song and guitar playing over its centuries of evolution from a genuine folk art to an almost classical fine art form.

The flamenco guitar differs from a classical one in many ways. Traditionally, its back and sides are either Spanish cypress, curly maple; its neck is Spanish cedar or a lightweight kind of mahogany; its woods are thinner; ebony pegs are used instead of tuning machines*, and its strings are set very low to the fingerboard and top. All of these features produce a lightweight instrument with minimum sustain but with a brightness and strong initial attack to each note. In addition, with the low action*, the percussive playing

JAMES FRIESON

James Frieson flamenco guitar. Back and sides of Lebanese cedar, top of Canadian western red cedar, fingerboard of ebony, bridge of rosewood. Body: 49cm. x 36.5cm. The capo strapped around the neck was also made by James from abalone shell, ivory, rosewood and felt.

*see glossary

The World of Musical Instrument Makers

techniques are made possible.

Jim has sometimes veered from tradition and used Lebanese cedar, cherry or pear for the backs and sides or, his preference for the tops, North American pine. He has found that the species of wood, assuming it has relatively similar characteristics, is not as crucial to the flamenco guitar's sound as is the age, method of drying and growth peculiarities of that particular wood.

JOHN: Mr. Laskin.....do you ever make flamenco guitars?

Yes I do. And I enjoy the challenge, but I dont' consider myself primarily a maker of flamencos. Jim, on the other hand, makes more flamencos than other types of guitars. Thus, more than any other guitar maker in the city, he is most deserving of a reputation as a flamenco maker. He has, however, made other instruments since he began his lutherie in 1977: mandolins, requintos, or smaller, higher pitched guitars, classical guitars and Appalachian dulcimers.

Jim has lived in Toronto since early 1974 when he left Ottawa, his birthplace. One of his first jobs here was in a production woodworking shop. It was, at the age of twenty-two, his first experience with woodworking. In that shop, employees were allowed to work on their own projects after business hours, thus providing Jim with the incentive to make himself the kind of guitar that he wanted but couldn't afford to buy. Although he had no background in working wood, Jim has been playing guitar since his early teens and has a natural artistic bent, both factors contributing to the feasibility of his guitar making attempt.

That first guitar, a classical, finished in 1974, was quickly followed by a second instrument made with the guidance of a 'how to' book. by this time, Jim realized he would need proper instruction if he wanted to progress fully into

instrument making. To this end, he searched for and eventually found the maker Olivo Chiliquinga with whom he worked for three and a half years. Over that period he gained experience at building and repairing a wide variety of stringed instruments.

Since 1980, he has been dividing his time between the restoration and refinishing of guitars, pianos, clocks, furniture and almost any wooden object, and the completion, on average, of one or two instruments each month.

MICHAEL: The finish seems slightly different on these guitars.

And so it should!

Jim is the only guitar maker in the city to use the traditional, hand rubbed, shellac french polish. He has become quite proficient at applying this tricky finish on everything from guitars and antique pianos to tables. His is a rare ability in Toronto. In comparison to other finishes, he much prefers the french polishing techniques and the shellac in particular. For him, it's faster than lacquers or varnishes, and the finish can be restored without the need of sanding or otherwise preparing the old coating to receive the new.

Some players and makers, Jim among them, strongly believe that especially for flamenco guitars, the thin shellac finish is a necessity for superior sound. In my own experience, I have found definite acoustic advantages to that kind of light finish on classical guitars as well. I won't however, open up the hornet's nest of instrument finishing opinions and theories. I'd rather take us across the room.

The next pair of instruments we will see, embody some of the most successfully innovative concepts and designs to have emerged from the violin making world and the field of musical instrument electronics. They are the unusually shaped items before you now.

15 Electric Violins, Violas, Cellos
Raad Instruments Incorporated

A small firm, a five way partnership known as Raad Instruments Inc., built this electric violin and cello. The unique shaping of body and scroll are but the first visual signs of a wholly original approach to electronic amplification.

Mounted on silver paint and epoxied or urethene-glued directly to the underside of the top in the instrument's heart area, i.e. in front of the bridge, is a thin polarized film. This film, unlike attachable ceramic pickups that behave in essence like microphones, mechanically follows the wood's own vibrations. When connected to a "Rolls-Royce" quality pre-amp* of their own design and manufacture, the end result is, to quote James Jones, one of the five partners, "a wonderful, magnificent violin, viola, cello or bass sound right at the jack* point" ie. without the need of mechanical equalizing* adjustments.

To enable their polarized film pickup to function in tandem with the vibrating top without amplifying unwanted resonances and noises, the top plate is not attached to the body. It floats on only two small isolators; one at the top of the frame, one at the bottom. With the top thus isolated from the body one would expect a subsequent loss of rigidity in the frame but that is compensated for by lining the sides and, in the cello, the back as well, with graphite fibres.

The backs of all Raad instruments are untraditionally flat but still made from traditional violin materials: curly or bird's eye maple or a fibre composite. The uniquely graduated top is made from any one of the major musical instru-ment spruces: sitka, German silver or Engelmann. The fingerboards and tailpieces are ebony.

Cellist Dick Armin, world patent holder of the Raad system's basic mechanical structure and floating-plate concept, stated their goal simply: "our whole idea is to be compatible with all the electronics available but with the true sound of the instrument".

MARTHA: I once saw a solid body electric violin. Wouldn't it do just as well?

Absolutely not. This also is where the Raad supercedes. Solid body electric violins with their typical magnetic pickups responding to the vibrating strings have, as Dick explained it, "no dynamic range. If you play loud and soft with the bow they really don't follow you." In addition, the sound quality is generally poor, brash and basically non violin-like, especially in response to the higher frequencies. As if that weren't bad enough, usual electric violins tend to feed back, produce a horrible howling if the player moves from a specific position in relation to the amplifier. Such a problem is nonexistent with a Raad.

SAMUEL: Their instruments appear to be around normal violin and cello size. Am I correct?

Yes. The scale length and general dimensions are indeed taken from traditional instruments. In fact, the makers chose very consiciously to build their designs on the same aesthetic principles that have guided violin makers since before Stradivari and to incorporate their new/old proportions as an integral part of their pickup system. Such elements as the top plate's thickness and shape or the body dimensions ae inseparably coupled with the mechanics of the pickup.Incidentally, an advantage of their shape is its allowance for freer hand positions higher up the fingerboard much like a cutaway guitar.

It's about time I told you of the people behind Raad Instruments and how their ideas came about.

The five equal partners I referred to earlier are Dick Armin, his brother Paul, their sister Adele Armin-Riley, James Jones and Jonathan Borah.

RAAD

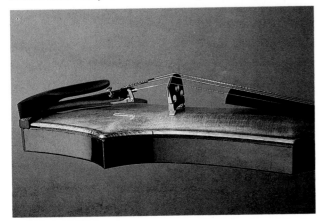

Raad violin. Detail showing "floating top" suspended on dense foam at points of the bouts and soft, breathable fill-in foam in between.

The World of Musical Instrument Makers

The Armins are a classically-trained musical family that spawned, at one point, the *Armin Electric String Quartet* with Dick on cello, Paul on viola, Adele on violin and one other brother, Otto, now a concertmaster in Germany, also playing violin. But it was Dick who initiated the search for a good electric pickup that culminated, after ten years of development, with their current design.

Born in Manitoba in 1944, Dick moved to Toronto by the mid 1960s to join in its healthy music scene. After a time as symphony cellist, curiosity about electro-acoustics lured him from the symphony and he joined the popular rock orchestra, *Lighthouse*. His first electric instrument in that band was a cello with a relatively primitive type *Kent* brand pickup attached. Not surprisingly, the inventive Mr. Armin grew dissatisfied with that and proceeded to have a solid body cello custom made for him that utilized a phonograph needle as a pickup

Not long after, the Barcus-Berry Company in the U.S. came out with the first ceramic pickups which vastly improved on previous pickups but still, to Dick's ear, were unable to amplify adequately many of the instrument's natural qualities. With determination to perfect the electro-acoustic sound, he followed up a lead about a thin film of sorts that a California frim was producing. Then began the decade of experimentation that drew on, in addition, the talents of four other people.

Paul Armin acts as the business manager of the company. Adele does all the musical public relations work demonstrating and performing on their instruments at important trade shows and violin world events regularly occurring in such cities as Paris, Nashville, Chicago, London and New York. Jonathan Borah is the builder, the woodworker and James Jones, an electronics engineer and bass player is, among other things,

the builder of the pickup technology and a co-patenter with Dick of their invented systems.

It was only after the five of them finally heard the sound they wanted, the results they had sought for ten years, that Raad Instruments was officially incorporated. They then commenced building prototypes and gearing up for production. That was in the winter of 1984.

Once their prototypes began surprising and exciting violin communities in both Europe and North America, they had their cue to start producing. In the last months of 1984 they reached a comfortable level of not more than ten instruments per month and have held themselves to that for the time being.

At present, their main electronics and testing labs, cluttered and packed as they are, the bench, floor and wall, with equipment, tools, circuitry components and the physical remnants of experiments, are in a small Vaughn Road building. The woodworking shop is in an industrial area further south and just east of downtown. Dick confided his intentions for the near future to have more of their separate facilities, including demonstration space, located under the Vaughn Road roof. That kind of consolidation should enable them to one day reach their intended production goal of 300 instruments yearly.

The Raad's critical success and growing acceptance into a very traditional and established instrument family is due not only to their respect for the old designs but also due to the fact that their electric instrument is not as crudely electric nor as offensive to an acoustic violinist as all other electric systems seem to be. The Raad spans the electro-acoustic gap so well because their pickup acts, as Dick concisely put it, "as a mechanical analogy of a natural occurrence. It is technically not electric!"

16 Classical Guitars
Kolya Panhuysen

Our next instrument is a classical guitar by Kolya Panhuysen, a nephew of the world-respected German guitar maker Edgar Monch.

Kolya was born in Berlin, Germany during the Second World War, in 1941. His family moved to Prague, Czechoslovakia for the last two years of the war while Berlin was being heavily bombed and then to Holland for eight years before emigrating to Canada in 1954 and heading almost immediately for Toronto.

Teaching was Kolya's original profession but while his Uncle Edgar was in Toronto for a six-year stint, Kolya enlisted his help in the building of a couple of guitars. Those two instruments, built in 1967 and 1968 and originally for his own use during guitar lessons, planted the seeds for his career change. In 1971, Kolya took a year's leave from teaching and spent it building guitars. After that, his choice of

KOLYA PANHUYSEN

career was made but it took a few years of half-time teaching, half-time making guitars and spending his summers in Mr. Monch's shop in Germany before he left teaching entirely. Kolya has been building guitars full time since 1977, making two or three instruments each month.

Although he has lately begun experimenting with his instrument building, he has readily emulated the designs and superior workmanship that defined the Monch style guitar, especially in light of Mr. Monch's untimely death in 1977. Most of Kolya's work is sold in Germany and Japan, but he has no intention of moving his home base from Toronto.

I know that you could probably tell me what materials Kolya built this guitar with. But please be patient and allow me.

The back and sides are Brazillian rosewood, the top is Cedar, the neck is tropical American

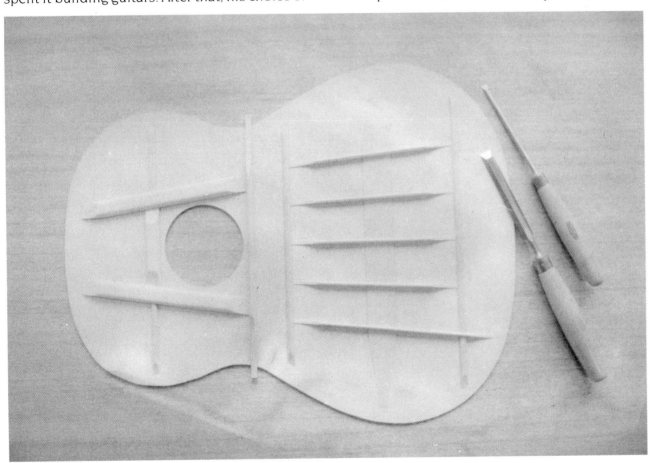

Kolya Panhuysen's braced classical guitar top ready for glueing onto a guitar body.

mahogany, the fingerboard is ebony, most likely from East India, and inside the guitar, for bracing of the top and back, Kolya used German and Sitka spruce.

LOUISE: You've mentioned the bracing before, Mr. Laskin, but when we look in the soundhole we can ony see the bars on the back. What does the bracing on the top look like?

Well, luckily, I have a photograph that shows what is on the underside of a Panhuysen top.

The bracing or strutting of a classical guitar top is traditionally based around some form of fan pattern where the delicate wooden bars within the lower bout* section, under the bridge, fan gently outward away from the soundhole and toward the bottom end of the guitar. More recent, scientifically designed bracing patterns possess bars of varying lengths and thickness that radiate outward in all directions from underneath the bridge area. There are almost as many varieties and interpretations of these basic approaches to top bracing as there are guitar makers, but so much evolution and thought has led up to both styles that they remain the standard upon which an individual maker's own ideas are based.

Did you have another question?

LOUISE: Yes. I was wondering . . . . how old an instrument is the guitar?

Oh my! That's a big subject. The guitar has a long history, but the modern, classical guitar emerged quite recently, in the 1850s.

Certain instruments have had the guitar label since as early as the 13th century, but it was the five-course or five doubled strings Vihuela of 16th century Spain that overshadowed its guitar style cousins and reigned throughout that century. For approximately the next 175 years a more guitar-like instrument, similar in its style of construction to a modern flat back and top guitar, still strung with only five courses, took and held the most popular spot. Then, after seventy-five more years of experimental building, the course of the developing guitar was changed by the pioneering work of Spain's Antonio de Torres Jurado.

During his first phase of guitar making, roughly from 1850 to 1869, Torres's innovative ideas involved enlarging the upper and lower bouts, deepening the sides, establishing the optimum basic string length of 65 centimetres and developing the original fan strutting that I just described. The combined effect of these radical alterations plus numerous aesthetic changes produced a guitar with a richer, stronger sound and better tonal response than any that had come before. It also took on the appearance and proportions of what has become the basis for the modern classical guitar.

In his downtown Toronto workshop, a converted, aging storefront, Kolya reflects strongly his own direct connection to the guitar making history of Europe. It is a link that he maintains by occasional year-long, working sabbaticals in Germany and his adherence to his Uncle's standard of work.

According to Kolya, the future may find him trying his luthier's hand at an Eastern European balalaika, a lute, a flamenco guitar or perhaps, all of the above.

DEBORAH: I've been noticing that many of these craftspeople use European woods such as German spruce, European maple and the like. I've never seen these woods in any of the lumberyards I've been to. Do instrument makers have to go to Europe themselves to buy it?

Not really. The sources and wholesalers of European musical instrument woods regularly deal by mail order so the materials can easily be imported. However, if you're able, it certainly does help to visit these suppliers yourself. Not only could you then pick through their stock and ensure yourself of receiving the maximum quality but personal contact always makes for a more dependable future business relationship.

MICHAEL: Have you ever gone to Europe yourself? For supplies that is.

Yes, once, To England and Germany.

Join me now at our next stop. We've another rarity awaiting us.

*see glossary

17 Lutes, Chitarrones
Michael Schreiner

Of the two lutes we're facing, both constructed by the lute and viol maker Michael Schreiner, it should be obvious which is the most rare. The unusually large lute, to be precise, 1.40 metres long, is actually called a chitarrone. This is Michael's copy of an instrument made in 1611 by the Italian maker Wendelin Tiffenbrucker or, as he has come to be known from the labelling of his instruments, Vvendelio Venere.

The bowl of the body and the elongated neck were made from yew wood, the top is German spruce and the fingerboard is ebony. With the large number of ribs, usually between twenty-five and thirty-five in this case twenty-six — in contrast to the more common nine to eleven that form the bowl on this style of lute, it earns the title multi-ribbed. The second pegbox at the top of the extension is where the eight diatonically* tuned bass strings are attached. Since the addi-tional bass strings were, of necessity, heavy and low pitched, the extended scale length was essential to maintain a proper tension.

Chitarrones or two-headed lutes as they are sometimes called, first appeared in the mid-1500s and retained their popularity for close to three centuries. In an effort to maximize the sound qualities to be gained from the long scaled basses, some makers were producing instruments almost two metres in length.

Michael's other lute, of renaissance style and tuned to A, was constructed with similar woods to the chittarone. This second lute is a more common type, but in view of the numerous styles that today's lute makers are asked to reproduce, it's difficult to clearly define common, as Michael indicated: "... take, for example, a seven-course lute. That means little of itself because you had long ones, thin ones, fat ones,

MICHAEL SCHREINER

Michael Schreiner renaissance lute. Detail of back showing the yew ribs and ebony/holly veneer strips on the neck. Also visible are the tied and knotted gut frets that wrap around the neck.

*see glossary

short ones, deep ones, and flat ones, and they were all different. Then you might have had ten courses of strings or thirteen or fourteen, or the different chitarrones. You have also the high pitched lutes like the A lute rather than the G lute or the F or D lute" — and Michael's twenty-eight different body moulds are proof of his statement. Apparently, what style of instrument a lute maker produces is determined sometimes by specific commission but more often by the current trend among lute players or other early music musicians.

EDITH: Is the lute an Italian instrument?

No, it isn't, but one might be encouraged to think so since Bologna, Venice, Padua and Rome were each, at different times, the predominant European lute-making centres. The lute was originally a four-string, plectrum-played Arabian instrument. It was introduced to Europe near the close of the 13th century. The Europeans were responsible for the instrument's development into the recognizable forms of the modern lutes like these of Michael's.

Michael came to Canada from Indiana in 1968. He settled for a time in Montreal, and it was while doing office work at McGill University that the need to build something overcame him. The many guitarists he knew influenced him to build a classical guitar for himself and he managed, in the space of a year and half and following a construction guide book, to do just that. He did confess that his home life was somewhat disrupted by his having no choice but to set up shop on their kitchen table then, day after day, clear everything away before the next meal.

Soon after, with the cumulative experience of two additional guitars, his decisive first lute was built which he traded for a friend's first harpsichord. Michael's wife at that time wanted a harpsichord and the harpsichord maker wanted a lute, so Michael's efforts were to satisfy them both. From that casual start, Michael has not looked back. With trial and error as his primary teachers, he has been building lutes ever since.

He has lived in Toronto since the early 1970s, and in 1976, with more than thirty lutes under his belt, Michael began a two year stint as the in-house lute builder at the workshop of Jean Larrivée. With the exception of that period, Michael has worked independently with, on occasion, one or two apprentice helpers of his own. Sandwiched in between constructing his lutes and more recently, viols, Michael has done guitar repair work, sold musical instrument woods and taught the instrument making course at the Ontario College of Art. Of all his sideline pursuits, teaching gives him the most pleasure and satifaction. For that reason he continues to teach out of his own workshop.

In spite of extra-curricular activities, he completes no fewer than thirteen to fifteen instruments per year and, if pushed for time, Michael is able to finish a simple basic lute in four or five days.

Seventeen years ago when Michael took his first guitar to a McGill music professor for constructive criticism, he was advised to "build twenty guitars as fast as you can, then you'll learn something about guitar making." Recently, he reflected on that advice, saying he'd "thought about how long it DID take to learn and I considered that only recently I'd reached a level of truly understanding the instruments." I asked Michael what sustained him through the intervening years, and he frankly replied: Oh: I love doing it!" Enough said.

In preparing this book, limiting myself to a maximum of two representative instruments posed more of a difficulty to some makers than to others. For the maker whose work we're now regarding, the restriction was almost severe.

Monti Egan, the craftsman responsible for this celtic harp and classical guitar, has also built five-string banjos, steel-string and electric guitars, mandolins, hammered dulcimers, thumb pianos and tongue drums. About two years ago Monti's preference for the classical guitar and harp emerged to take precedence over his instrument endeavors. That, at least, made his choice easier.

Many of the makers we've seen so far were self-taught, as was Monti, and many of those began with a guitar but soon switched to some other instrument(s). Monti adds a new twist to the pattern. Although he plays the guitar and has been in various bands and has studied classical guitar in England, the instrument that resulted from his initial motivation toward stringed instrument constructing was a celtic harp. In 1971, after hearing Alan Stivell, Brittany's most renowned harpist, Monti was enchanted. For three months he researched the harp and its construction and finally made one of himself.

He has been a woodworker since his childhood, making such things as speaker cabinets and furniture. So building that first harp and becoming a full-time instrument maker was, as Monti put it, "a logical extension" for his life. He was "always making something".

Born in St. Catharines, Ontario, he grew up in Calgary. He came to Toronto in 1973 and satisfied his need, made apparent after a tour of Europe, to live in a more exciting city. It's here, in the rear section of his High Park home, that he has been building full-time since 1979. In addition to some financially necessary repairwork, he finishes approximately twenty instruments a year.

His classical guitar was made with the traditional proper woods that you've come to know: East Indian rosewood, western red cedar, mahogany and ebony. His harp, an instrument uncommon among the city's makers, uses mahogany for its body, pillar i.e. the "T" cross piece and neck or harmonic curve where the tuning pins attach, and cedar for its soundboard. Monti also uses maple or oak for harp bodies and frames and spruce for the tops.

This particular celtic harp is very near to as full a size as the celtic harps reached. It has thirty metal strings tuned diatonically and beginning, in this instance, from a low C note two octaves below middle C.

Although Monti devotes the larger part of his attention to his classical guitars, I surmise that at this point in our tour you're more interested in the harp. I'm glad. That gives me leave to tell you more about it.

The playing of harp instruments is recorded as far back in history as 3000 B.C. but the first Irish reference, being representative of the Celtic countries in general, was 2,500 years later — in 541 B.C. The frame harp, with its pillar to give the neck support against the strings' tension, replaced the bent-bow style of harp where the strings themselves pulled the frame into the "c" shape and appeared in Britain during the 8th century. From that time and until the middle ages, Irish, Scottish and Welsh harpers enjoyed a position of importance and respectability. Although, according to the contemporary American harpist Robin Williamson, "with the coming of Christianity, the invasions of the Vikings and social disruption and feuding in the British Isles, the harpers lost much of their influence and power".It was primarily the efforts, in the 10th century of the Irish

MONTI EGAN

Monti Egan classical guitar. Back view showing E. Indian rosewood back and sides, mahogany neck. Body: 49.5cm. x 36.2cm.

hero and king, Brian Boru that ensured the celtic harp's revived popularity for half a millennium and its continued fundamental association with Ireland.

Celtic harps were strung with brass and steel wire until the end of the 18th century when the gut-strung neo-celtic harp prevailed. It was the neo-celtic harp — now strung with nylon — that became the more popular choice of harpists in this century's enduring celtic music revival. It has only been in the last decade that the ancient metal string versions have been revived as well. Monti's harp, as is evident, emulates the earlier style.

GARY: What's the difference between the celtic harp and the one used for classical music?

Well, for a start, modern, classical harps are much larger, in some instances standing taller than the player, and have greater musical ranges due to the addition of as many as twenty strings, primarily in the lower register. Another obvious difference in the classical harp is the row of pedals at its base. Where the celtic harp often has what are called sharping levers which, when manually turned or flipped sideways, press against the string and raise its pitch slightly, thus obtaining the semitone, the classical harp's pedals actuate similar acting hook mechanisms, or fourchettes, by means of link-rods placed inside the straightened pillar and neck. The concert classical harpist is able, by means of the pedals, to alter the pitch of any string by as much as a full tone.

Although Monti often installs sharping mechanisms on his harps, he intentionally excluded them this time, once again in imitation of the earlier instruments.

With the work of the next maker on the tour, you'll be able to add, among other things, a third and different approach to your experience of the styles of flute making in the city.

19 Recorders, Wooden Flutes
Peter Noy

You'll recall that I've already mentioned Peter Noy in reference to his aiding his friend Mr. Shoebridge in the design of the procelain flutes.

The two instruments that Peter has chosen from his woodwind making repertoire are an alto recorder and an Irish flute. The flute being, in Peter's words, "essentially of an early 19th century concert type" that is used most often for playing Irish and British folk music. It is made from stained boxwood, a wood that Peter particularly likes for its tone and workability.

The recorder also is made from boxwood and, like the flute, its fittings are shaped from imitation ivory.

MICHAEL: Can I assume that Peter turned these instruments?

You certainly can.

All cylindrical woodwind instruments are turned on a lathe at some point in their manufacture.

With this recorder, constructed in the baroque fashion, Peter turns separately each of the three sections — the head joint, main-joint and foot-joint.

The drilled and shaped hollow centres of any woodwind instrument, correctly called the bore, is an equally if not more crucial aspect of their construction. For example, in this recorder the bore tapers, getting slightly narrower as it nears the bottom end. If this was a Renaissance recorder, the bore would have a wider taper making the instrument louder but limiting its musical and tonal range.

But for a simple Renaissance flute with its straight cylindrical bore, the conical bores of the recorders and later flutes, like this one, are necessary to keep the instrument in proper tune as the higher octaves are played. The increased air speed needed to produce the higher notes

PETER NOY

Peter Noy at his lathe turning the bottom of a tenor recorder.

would flatten the higher octaves if not for the adjusting effects of the taper.

A final critical process of these instruments' fabrication is the spacing and sizing of the finger holes. Peter begins with small openings and gradually increases their size until they are in tune. The finger holes are thus accurately adapted to the bore of each instrument.

MICHEAL: How does Peter know which bore taper will be correct and in tune for a given instrument?

That's simple.

There are historical records of measurements used that he can refer to, or he could measure a museum piece for himself. Once he possesses that data, he fine-tunes, evolving his own more accurate scales and tuning with the use of an electronic signal generator.

Peter came to Toronto from the Barrie and Orilla, Ontario area in 1969 to attend the University of Toronto. As a result of his lifetime enjoyment of music, he started to play the recorder in 1971 when he was twenty-one years old and became curious about its construction. To satisfy his curiosity, he attended an early instrument making class at Scarborough College organized by the Toronto Consort, an early music performance group.

At the same time, he was developing an interest in Irish folk music. He "fell in love with Irish folk music's liveliness, freedom and high standards of musicianship". He then began teaching himself to play the "Irish style" flute, it was almost inevitable that Peter would purchase a lathe and begin experimenting. Since there were no local makers with whom he could apprentice, he faced the "blind alleys of self-teaching" with the help of current and historical woodwind instrument building guides and the advice of any other makers he met.

Beginning in 1977, he made hundreds of wooden flageolets, numerous maple prototypes of flutes and recorders and dozens of finished, professional quality instruments. This methodical learning process spanned four years but its ultimate success encouraged Peter to become a full-time maker. He has been just that ever since.

In a studio on the Toronto Islands, using coco-bolo and curly maple in addition to the boxwood, Peter annually completes close to twenty instruments. Included among them are baroque tenor and Renaissance soprano recorders, Renaissance flutes of all sizes such as soprano to bass, and baroque flutes as well as instruments like the two in this show.

These steel string guitars are all three as different as day and night. You'll easily recognize the style of the first one; it's a cutaway flat-top. The second one is known as an arch-top or for obvious reasons, an f-hole guitar. It brings to five the number of guitar styles represented in the show. The third is a complex totally customized instrument, with four different sets of strings, that Linda Manzer, the maker of all these guitars, calls *Pikasso*. Linda had been primarily a flat-top steel guitar maker until recently, when she followed her love of jazz guitar playing into the world of the arch-top.

Towards the end of the 19th century, a shoe clerk and would-be instrument maker, Orville Gibson, adapted to his own guitars and mandolins the violin making procedure of carving the top and back. His aim was to improve on the inadequacies he perceived in the guitars and mandolins of his day by borrowing successful features from a more perfected acoustic instrument. He succeeded to such a degree that making instruments became a full-time business that grew, eight years later, into The Gibson Company. Gibson is also credited as being one of the first professional guitar makers in North America to use metal strings.

Because steel string guitars of all types evolved first from the arched instruments of Orville Gibson and soon after, from the more traditional unarched, in most cases, guitars of C.F. Martin and Co., the term flat-top emerged to differentiate between them.

In the early 1930's, in New York City, an arch-top maker named John D'Angelico began making what many musicians feel were among the finest jazz guitars ever built. His principal apprentice and co-worker, Jim D'Aquisto, has

LINDA MANZER

Linda Manzer. Detail of customized instrument Linda dubbed Pikasso. It contains one conventional 6-string steel string guitar, a short scale fretless 12-string guitar plus two separate additional sets of 12 strings: one tuned to a chord and available for strumming, the other existing to sympathetically pick up and enhance vibrations from the other strings.

perpetuated those standards since his teacher's death in 1964 and is the man who taught Linda her arch-top building skills.

Linda has played guitar since she was twelve years old. At that time, in 1965, she made herself an electric guitar by sawing chunks off an acoustic guitar and gluing on wings to imitate the electric then popular. Her next instrument making venture happened six years later while attending Sheridan College just outside Toronto. She built two Appalachian dulcimers* — one from a kit, a second from scratch — then made a bowed-lyre form of instrument called a crwth.

After graduating from the College with a Creative Arts degree, affirming her proficiency in woodworking, photography and animation, Linda gave little thought to instruments until her travels landed her in the wood shop of an art and design college in Nova Scotia. Someone there was making a guitar and the idea that she could do the same was born.

In the search for a guitar maker who could and would teach her, Jean Larrivée's name surfaced. To Linda, he was soon to become more than just a name for she spent the next three and a half years working for him in his Toronto and Victoria workshops.

Since first setting out to make her own instruments in the late seventies, Linda has seen her cutaway guitars played by, among others, Pat Metheny, her favourite guitarist.

Although she had years of full-time building experience behind her she temporarily, early in 1984, became an apprentice once more. That was when she spent four months with Jim D'Aquisto in his New York shop acquiring the specialized skills for arch-top building that a flat-top guitar maker wouldn't know.

Still fairly new to arch-top making but now, firmly back in her own Cabbagetown workshop, this particular arch-top of Linda's reflects many of D'Aquisto's concepts. It is, in fact, patterned after one of D'Aquisto's *New Yorker* models. She carved the back from a solid piece of curly maple; the top from German spruce; the neck is curly maple and ebony was used for the fingerboard, bridge, tailpiece and pickguard.

Linda's flat-top instruments use the rosewood, spruce, ebony and mahogany with which you are very familiar.

DEBORAH: Mr. Laskin? Why is it that certain woods seem to be so common to certain instruments that we're able to become, as you say, familiar with them?

Generally, the same woods are used within instrument families because they have proven to give the best performance in their given roles.

Throughout years of experimentation and refinement, woods and other materials acoustically or structurally inferior were discarded until makers were left with the ones in current use.

This is not to say that a wood with similar properties might not do just as well in a given circumstance. A good example of that is the use of other softwoods such as redwood, fir, cedar or pine in place of spruce for the soundboards of guitars and violins. Once a maker has accounted for the stiffness strength to weight ratio, etc. — she/he could, with the proper adaptations, enable one soundboard wood to equal the response of another while retaining its own distinctive qualities.

No two people hear the same thing exactly the same way, nor do they, subconsciously or consciously, want to hear the same things. Similarly, no two players seem to want precisely the same qualities in a instrument. So, once the structural needs can be met, variations in the subtler tonal responses are one possible way of better meeting the desires of an individual musician.

Such variations are, as I've explained, rarely far from established norms for the wood types that best suit the different parts on an instrument, at least, not with much success.

It's time to move on to our twenty-first stop.

*see glossary

21 Steel Drums
Steeltone Musical Co. Ltd., — Ed Peters and Michael Salvador

As we were admiring in the first gallery the steelpans made by Earle Wong you'll recall I explained the instrument's relative newness and hence its unmet need for refinement and standardization.

The steelpan work of Ed Peters and Michael Salvador, under their business name Steeltone Musical Company Limited, is a serious response to that need. Their more judicious application of acoustical physics to the pan's construction has resulted in measurably more musical notes.

If you'll bear with me, untrained acoustical physician that I am, I'll try to explain briefly the gist of Ed's and Michael's improvements.

Their investigations show that the primary audible sounds in a traditionally made pan's note are the vibrating frequencies of the note itself and its Anharmonics*. But due to the way in which Ed and Michael delineate the note areas on their drums, one can hear not only the note and its anharmonic modes* but its harmonic modes* as well.

The subtle manipulation of the different modes, that in various combinations comprise every musical sound, is the means they have found to produce a purer note. As a result of their control of the acoustics, their anharmonic modes decay faster and their harmonic modes last longer, thus becoming predominant as the note fades.

GARY: How do they...

Hold on. I know what you are going to ask but I was just about to tell you so stay with me.

If you look closely at one of the pans, constructed, incidentally, from 45-gallon steel oil drums — as is common, you'll notice that the shapes of the sectioned-out notes on the face are not the usual tapering U's or small circles and elipses. On a Steeltone pan the bottom curves of the U have been squared off and the elipses have become rectangles. This is the visible evidence of Ed's and Michael's method of allowing the note to occupy the precise area on the drum that it needs, an area whose size has been pre-calculated following the laws of physics. This is in opposition to the traditional method of oversizing the note's area then tightening the note, in the centre of that area in an effort to fine tune.

Ed had not begun serious tuning until soon after coming to Canada in 1963, but as a teenager in his native Trinidad, he had already made some cursory attempts. Like other kids who couldn't afford real drum sets, Ed amassed a collection of 48-ounce juice tins — forty four at one point — and tried to tune them apportioning one note per can.

Ed is now a high school geography teacher. About one year into his studies at Montreal's Sir George Williams University toward that career goal, he began teaching himself to properly tune the oil drums. As a necessary prerequisite to outfitting his first Canadian band, Ed had to be able to tune. So, using as guinea pigs the first couple of oil drums he acquired and working from memories of Trinidadian tuners he had observed, he tried, erred, tried again and in the process learned to tune.

From that time, including his partnership with Michael since 1980, Ed has made or helped make a minimum of 250 complete instruments comprising over 600 separate pans.

Like Ed, Michael is a steelpan player, has been for over twenty years, and he too came to Canada from Trinidad to study. Michael graduated from Waterloo University as an electrical engineer and is now employed by Ontario Hydro. As a player, he became frustrated with the inadequacies of the instrument and decided to investigate ways of improving it by applying the rules of physics that govern other musical instruments. He teamed up with Ed shortly thereafter and the refined Steeltone pan ultimately resulted.

At present, there is a patent pending on their new type of steelpans, and they intend to introduce them to players back in Trinidad as the more challenging part of a larger marketing scheme.

GARY: Are these pans always made from big oil drums?

Yes, I'd say so.

GARY: So they're always steel?

STEELTONE

The World of Musical Instrument Makers

Ah…There I can qualify my yes.

Sometimes, finished steel pans have been plated with brass, bronze, or chrome. It is done for aesthetic reasons and has no discernible effect on the sound.

Ed proudly describes the steelpans as constituting the only complete percussive family of instruments, enabling, as I mentioned in connection with Earle Wong, whole orchestras of them to be established. Consequently, Ed and Michael have also organized both an adult and a youth orchestra as non-profit corporations. Ironically, these orchestras still require traditional drums for percussion because the steel drum has become so musical.

Leaving the percussive, we return to the plucked as we commence our appreciation of the splendid variety of stringed instruments that will see us through to the concluding display of the exhibition.

The first of these is immediately to your left.

This classical guitar was built by the man who shares Kolya Panhuysen's workshop, Robin Green.

EDITH: There seem to be a lot of guitar makers in Toronto.

There are. Not as many as there are lawyers but relative to other instrument makers, more guitarmakers are working in Toronto than in any other single metropolitan area on the continent! As a matter of fact, Toronto is referred to as guitar town in the halls of Chicago's school of violin making.

MARTHA: Wow, like wouldn't it be great bein' a guitar maker?

Well I can't disagree with you there.

MARTHA: I mean like, all the neat wood…, and nothing' to worry about…, just comin' in to work whenever ya feel like it. Must be nice.

I really don't want to discourage you but it's not all roses, if you know what I mean. One is at the mercy of events that one cannot always control — humidity, temperature and the variations and imperfections in natural materials.

MARTHA: Y'mean 'cause the wood might crack?

Essentially, yes. But that is not all of it. Try placing yourself in the position of an artisan who has carefully and properly seasoned his or her wood, a process that often takes years, then painstakingly fashioned it to precise dimensions and shape only to uncover, with the final chisel stroke, a tiny unsightly knot or hidden hairline crack rendering the piece unusable. All of the work will have been for naught.

MARTHA: Has that ever happened to you?

More often than I would have liked.

I once had an even worse experience…..

An earlier workshop of mine was in a little turn-of-the-century commercial building since demolished. The building was so ramshackle that no insurance company would cover it for burglary — it was too easy to break into. They suggested I get a dog instead.

It was a body-rub studio before I moved in — "Sexy Sacha's Spas" — and I found the red, black and orange felt wallpaper too difficult to paint over so I left it alone. In a dungeon-like basement lived the original oil furnace placed there in 1900. As the core of the hot water/radiator heating system, this furnace leaked and evaporated its total water supply every two days. Needless to say, if I wanted continuous heat, going away for more than a weekend involved elaborate preparations.

At the end of one particular January workday, a completed guitar neck, ready for the finishing process, lay on my bench. The neck was part of a special guitar, so as well as completing the shaping, I had inlaid a floral pattern on the peghead, carved a design into the heel and capped the heel with ivory. I left for dinner satisfied with my day's work.

At 2:00 a.m., on my way home from an evening out, I dropped by the shop to discover cold radiators and a temperature of 55 degrees farenheit and dropping. A quick check of the furnace showed plenty of water but NO OIL. The fuel company forgot to deliver. You can imagine the difficulty I had getting an emergency oil delivery after two o'clock on a cold January morning when the rest of the world seemed also to have run out of oil.

I remember pacing the cold shop for three hours until a fuel tanker showed up and another hour and a half while the radiator brought the temperature back to normal. Finally, by 7:00 a.m. I was home in my bed.

I awoke five hours later thinking that at least

the worst had passed and I had a story I could laugh about. I felt differently once I returned to the shop.

There on the bench was the special neck with a gaping, cavernous crack running the length of the mahogany and three of four additional cracks riddling the ebony fingerboard on the opposite side. The too abrupt temperature changes of warm – cold – warm had overstressed the dense ebony by not allowing it the time to adjust gradually. Thus, the damage was caused, leaving the neck a total write-off.

I was so angry at my bad luck that I picked up the now useless neck and threw it down the long narrow corridor that fed the four separate rooms of my shop. I quickly ran down the corridor, retrieved the neck, threw it back then ran back, picked it up and threw it the length a third time.

With my frustration more or less dissipated, I began re-making the neck, extras and all.

About four days later the new neck was ready to begin the finishing. When I left for the day I checked the oil level just to be sure. It was three-quarters full.

Next morning, arriving for work, I stared in disbelief at another cracked neck. I was dumbfounded. My mind was numbed but it seemed as if my body didn't miss a beat. I watched as my hands reached for more raw materials and began to build the neck a third time.

With hindsight, I realized that the woods in my shop had not had time to re-adjust to room temperature. The ebony and mahogany still had more and differing degrees of contracting to do when I went ahead and clamped them in place. I should have waited a few more days.

On the morning after the third neck was completed I was so afraid of discovering another disaster that I barely mustered the courage to go into my main workroom and look on the bench. Once in the shop and only after I sent on ahead of me a commiserating friend, I literally slithered along the corridor wall until I reached the entrance to the aforementioned workshop. Slowly I then peeked around the door frame until the neck came into view.

Miracle of miracles; no cracks were visible! My steps were tentative as I approached the bench to examine the neck more closely. I had to inspect it over and over before I became convinced of the truth. This one had made it!

Ironically, about eight years after the neck incident, that particular guitar was ruined in a car accident and the unsalvagably damaged guitar body had to be replaced. The neck however, suffered nary a scratch.

Robin Green is a second generation Canadian and a Toronto native. He taught high school math and science before turning to guitarmaking but woodworking in general was not new to him. It was, in fact, architectural model building, cabinetwork and renovation jobs that financed his university education.

When he met the guitarmaker, Kolya Panhuysen, who himself had not yet left full-time teaching, Robin allowed himself to be talked into attempting a guitar. With his woodworking skills already developed, what intrigued Robin was the additional dimension to the woodworked object that guitarmaking could provide — music! So in the spring of 1977 at the age of twenty-seven, he began spending his evenings and weekends in Mr. Panhuysen's shop learning guitarmaking.

It took a year and a half of teaching by day and making guitars by night before Robin convinced himself that the luthier's trade did indeed bring him the satisfaction he failed to realize from teaching. At that moment, he quit teaching and has been making guitars full time ever since. He continues to share space with his friend and teacher Mr. Panhuysen but, as is also true for his shopmate, the work on his yearly eighteen or twenty guitars is entirely his own.

Occasionally, Robin is still called on to build an architectural model or two, a craft he continues to enjoy, but his preference, by far, is the musical instruments.

Although making his first guitar is an often recalled complete high, for Robin, "the real sustenance of guitarmaking is in the little satisfactions of day-to-day work". The artisan's lifestyle is particularly appealing to him. "All I have to deal with all day is wood and myself," he says.

Robin's guitar was built primarily, as ex-

Robin Green at his workbench.

pected, with Brazillian rosewood, German spruce, ebony and mahogany. I know you are well familiar with these materials for guitar construction but keep in mind that though common to the guitars in this exhibition, these are not the only materials a guitar may be built from . These became the traditional choices simply because they proved to be the best through the process of elimination I spoke about earlier. A hand maker who wishes to always make the best possible guitar (as most do) will obviously choose not to waste his or her efforts on inferior materials. Robin is no exception.

EDITH: When you said the next instruments we'd see were stringed it made me curious about the strings themselves. Do you know how they're made?

I can briefly explain the process to you but before I do, some historical background might be helpful.

The substance from which the treble strings on Robins's guitar were made is a monofilament nylon produced originally for fishing line that has only been available for use since Second World War. Prior to that and since ancient times, strings were made either of spun sheep's intestines, hence gut strings, floss silk or, since the mid-14th century, drawn wire of steel or brass.

The process of overwrapping a core string with metal began in the 17th century and is still the method necessary for strings to achieve the lower vibrating pitches.

Metal strings beginning as thick rods, were both made into wire and produced in differing diameters by drawing the rod through successively smaller holes in a drawplate made from a harder metal. That process still forms the basis for the manufacture of modern metal strings. Today a desired diameter is achieved by mechanically drawing the wire through a series of dies.

This drawn wire, most commonly Swedish steel coated with tin, is then left plain or wrapped with other drawn wire of bronze, brass or a nickel alloy. On Robin's guitar, the bass strings have nylon-floss cores with an outer wire wrapping of nickel-silver.

The winding or overwrapping process is done either on an automatic winding machine or by hand. On the machine, the tightly stretched core is revolved 25,000 times per minute while a moving arm feeds the overwrap wire strand onto the core. The hand winding process, where human arms replace the mechanical one, is used for nylon core strings such as classical guitar basses.

While you are disgesting aspects of musical instrument string manufacturing, let me lead you to the next exhibit.

ANASTAS FOTEV

The viola here beside me was built by the Bulgarian-born and trained violin maker and restorer Anastas Fotev. It was constructed with what Anastas feels are the best woods for bowed instruments: German spruce, Yugoslavian curly maple and, of course ebony.

Of the European curly maples and sycamores, Anastas chooses those from Yugoslavia for geographical reasons. The length of seasons south of the Alps naturally affect tree growth and ring* configuration, hence, its sound-producing capabilities, in a way more beneficial to the wood's vibrating properties than if it originated north of the Alps.

For the same reasons, Anastas feels the best of the North American curly maple is to be found south of the Canadian Rockies, in the state of Oregon.

On the subject of wood Anastas has much to say. Not only does he believe that an eight year period of natural air drying is a necessity for violin woods but also that the parent tree's initial felling must happen in the winter months and only during a full moon. That may sound unusual at first, but there is a rational basis to such beliefs.

A serious problem common to old violins is the damage done by tiny burrowing insects and worms. The pits, holes and otherwise corrosive results of their endeavours can at best negatively affect the sound and at worst physically weaken an instrument. By felling a tree during the full moon, you have caught it at a point in a natural cycle when the sap is underground. The resulting lumber will then contain minimal amounts of the chemical constituents that attracts the worms. thus, you prevent any present or future insect damage.

Anasta Fotev viola. Yugoslavian curly maple, German spruce, ebony. 68.5cm. x 24.2cm.

*see glossary

Anastas learned his craft in the newly established violin making school in Plovdiv. In 1952, at the age of fifteen, he began the required eight years of training that resulted in his ability to make all bowed instruments and their bows, as well as to build guitars and repair pianos. Of those eight years, Anastas spent the first five at the school, and the remaining three at a compulsory apprenticeship. He was one of the school's first graduates, and five years later, in 1965, he enjoyed another personal first.

In that year, communist Bulgaria began offering permits that allowed one to be a private craftsperson or artist, and Anastas had the good fortune to be among the first wave of recipients.

The benefits of that small, progressive step proved, within a couple of years, to have limitations still. As a result, Anastas' plans for the near future began focusing on North America. His emigration to Canada in late 1968 was the end result of managing to leave Bulgaria, countless months of waiting and finally, in Vienna, Austria, receiving Canadian government sponsorship.

Almost immediately on arrival in Toronto, he was hired as a repairman by George Heinl and Co., one of the most respected violin dealerships in the country. But for a craftsman who had already run his own shop, employee status was difficult to abide. This burning need to have his own business and deal directly with the public was not to be met for five years.

It was only after working two years for Heinl, two years for Remenyi House of Music, another large firm, and doggedly improving his English

with the help of Seneca College that Anastas realized his goal of self-employment. His first business was established on Bathurst Street in 1974.

Through Bathurst Street and succeeding shops, Anastas earned his Toronto reputation of being a master repairer, restorer and maker of concert quality instruments. His violins are played by performers throughout the continent, including Stephen Staryck, concert master for the Toronto Symphony.

In the past year, Anastas began concentrating more on building the instruments and limiting his repair and restoration work to select clients. His goal is to complete an instrumental quartet — two violins and the companion viola and cello.

DEBROAH: Exactly how is a viola tuned?

In fifths* as a violin but one fifth lower. Its first string, an A, corresponds to a violin's second string.

It is interesting to note that as a result of the slightly lower pitch of the viola's tuning and the conflicting need of its players for the ease of a relatively short scale, closer to that of the higher pitched violin, the instrument is still thought of as an imperfect hybrid. Some experts feel the instrument is too small to adequately respond to a note one fifth below a violin. Others believe that if constructed to proper dimensions the viola would be unwieldy and have a wrong sound. The controversy has yet to be definitively concluded.

*see glossary

JOE LADO

Although solid body electric guitars did not emerge until after World War II, electrically amplified guitars have been commercially available in one form or another since the early 1930s.

The first successful electric guitar was an aluminum Hawaiian guitar made by the Rickenbacher company in 1931. It was amplified by the first effective electromagnetic pickup. For the next one and a half decades, electric guitars remained essentially acoustic guitars with pickups. It was not until the experiments of guitarist and innovator, Les Paul in the early forties and later the work of two other independent Californians — Paul Bigbsy and Leo Fender — that the modern solid body electric came into being.

GARY: Is that the same Les Paul that the Gibson guitar company had named models after?

It is. In fact it was Les Paul himself who badgered Gibson into producing, with his assist-ance, their first solid body electric guitars. As a result they rightfully bore the name *Les Paul Model.*

As well as helping to create the solid body electric guitar, this inventive musician was the originator of multi-track recording, or the process of overlapping separate recorded layers of sound onto the same tape without erasing the previous track, but that is a story for another time.

The creative person whose work should now command our attention is Joseph Kovacic also known as Joe Lado and for a while, as Joe strings. He, plus three full-time and three part-time workers, was responsible for these electric guitars.

Lado Musical Inc., Joe's company, builds solid body electrics, guitars and basses, from exotic hardwoods such as zebrawood, padauk and bird's-eye maple. The necks are always a three-piece laminate of maple/padauk or rosewood/maple — to prevent warping — and the

Joe Lado solid body electric guitars. The coloured, lacquered and airbrushed bodies are made from zebrawood, padauk or bird's-eye maple. The necks are a laminate of maple/padauk or rosewood/maple.

fingerboards are most often rosewood. The majority of Joe's guitars contain pickups designed specifically for his instruments by a California firm.

Joe's impressively varied instrument-making past began in his native Yugoslavia at the age of thirteen. He was accepted as an apprentice at the Zagreb school of guitar making on the recommendation of an uncle who was at that time, foreman of a large guitar making shop. That apprenticeship lasted for five years, until 1963, and entailed, apart from learning guitar making, numerous six-month intervals of concentrating, one at a time, on instruments as varied as accordions and violins. As well, Joe was taught the process of fabricating musical instrument hardware such as fretwire and machine heads.

Two years after graduating, he settled in Vienna and amassed a wealth of experience by working first for a violin maker, then for the piano maker Hugo Shtelchamer and ultimately for the reputable Crossman Guitar Works.

The subject of Canada had been a constant one throughout Joe's years of schooling. It was inevitable then that he would decide to give it a try. He came here in 1968, the same year that Anastas Fotev emigrated. Like Anastas, Joe's first years were spent in the employ of a large firm, in this case, Turner Musical Instruments.

Before 1970 expired, Joe had left Turner and set up his first shop in a Gerrard Street basement. The nickname Joe Strings originated with this shop. In the succeeding years, Joe moved his shop to various locations around Metro Toronto and once out to the nearby town of Uxbridge.

The Uxbridge shop immediately preceded his current location in Toronto's easternmost borough. It was in Uxbridge that his production, with the help of eighteen employees, hit a peak of thirty guitars a week. But after five years of working at that level, Joe decided to return to Toronto and to a more modest approach.

With his smaller shop, he produces approximately twelve electric instruments a month. They find homes in all of the countries of Europe and Scandinavia, as well as Israel, Japan and Australia. Somehow, amongst the electrics and repairwork, Joe finds the time to construct an occasional acoustic guitar and some five-string banjos. He confided his intention to squeeze in four or five mandolins each year as well!

To those of you who have assumed we'd already run the gamut of the various types of Toronto-made instruments I say, "not so fast!" Once you've had your fill of Lado guitars let us have an ethnic taste of the Mediterranean....

25 Bouzoukis, Classical Guitars
Constantin Tingas

CONSTANTIN TINGAS

The work of Athens-born Constantin Tingas spans three distinct instrument families. He builds violins and cellos, guitars and each member of the Greek bouzouki family: the lauto or simply, lute, the bouzouki itself, the joura, the baglama or the smallest and the related lute-guitar. His diverse output is represented here by a classical guitar and, unique in the show, a bouzouki.

MARTHA: Hey!… Great!…I love it! Did ya ever look inside his bouzouki?

I know what you are seeing. Among bouzouki makers it is a tradition to completely cover the inside of the bowl with silver or gold metallic paper.

MARTHA: And the neck's jet black! It looks like plastic.

You have just spotted another modern construction tradition. The neck has indeed been wrapped in unfinished black plastic. Bouzouki players find this style of neck offers less drag to their playing than finished wood.

Constantin's lutherie, augmented on occasion with furniture woodcarving, a skill he picked up in the workshop next door to his grandfather's, and the repairing of Greek instruments, has been his primary occupation ever since. From his cluttered, well-used shop in the basement of his east end home, he annually produces at least twenty of the different Greek instruments as well as varying number of guitars and bowed instruments. In 1983, for example, apart from Greek lutes, bouzoukis and jouras, Constantin completed fourteen guitars and two cellos.

Although Constantin developed the bulk of his luthier's skills under his grandfather's supervision, his first instrument, completed in 1959 at the age of fifteen, was built during a sixteen-

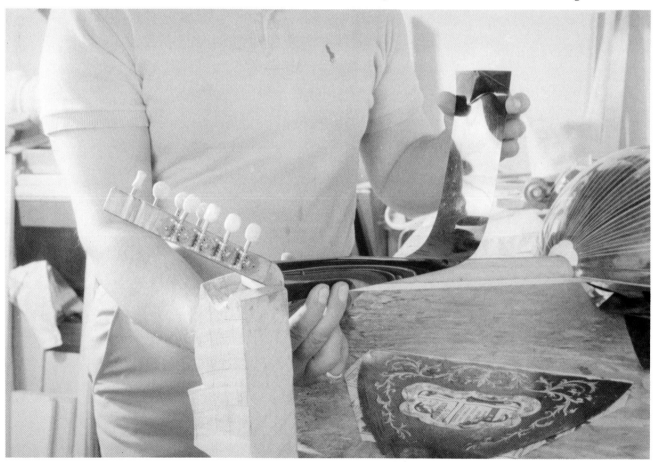

Constantin Tingas demonstrating the covering of a bouzouki neck with plastic sheeting.

month term at the International School of Violin Making in Verona, Italy. While still a teenager, Constantin also had the pleasure of spending a couple of months in Paris working with the world-renowned guitar maker, Robert Bouchet who happened to be a family friend.

When he was twenty-three and already tiring of unstable Greek politics, Constantin emigrated to Canada. For climatic reasons, his first stop was Vancouver, but within one year he had come east and enrolled in aeronautical engineering at the University of Toronto.

In 1971, three years into his university studies and one year switching from engineering to architecture, Constantin chose to spend his available summer setting up a shop and building instruments. That shop (on Adelaide St.) and its inherent satisfactions must have awakened his dormant luthier's spirit for he decided, by summer's end, to continue with it full time.

Constantin's lutherie, augmented on occasion with furniture woodcarving, a skilled he picked up in the workshop next door to his grandfather's, and the repairing of Greek instruments, has been his primary occupation ever since. From his cluttered, well-used shop in the basement of his east end home, he annually produces at least twenty of the different Greek instruments as well as varying number of guitars and bowed instruments. In 1983, for example, apart from Greek lutes, bouzoukis and jouras, Constantin completed fourteen guitars and two cellos.

EDITH: Was the bouzouki invented by Greeks? Not solely.

The modern bouzouki, the type in use for the last couple of centuries, did evolve in Greece, dovetailing unusually well into that country's living folk tradition. But it had emerged from a larger family of plectrum instruments prevalent throughout what was then the Ottoman Empire.

Today, in Arab lands formerly under Ottoman rule, there is a similar long-necked, bowl-bodied instrument known as a buzuk. Present-day Turkey also retains its own bouzouki-like instrument, the saz, as clear proof of the Greek bouzouki's interrelated history.

For this particular bouzouki, Constantin used walnut and maple to form the ribs of the bowl and spruce for the top. Beneath the plastic, the neck is a three-piece laminate with basswood glued to either side of a padauk centrepiece.

On his classical guitar Constantin, as with most guitarmakers, has used the East Indian rosewood, spruce, mahogany and ebony we would expect. On occasion, however, Constantin finds that by using a Brazillian wood, Pau ferro, for the back and sides, he is able to bring out certain sound qualities he describes as "somewhere between a flamenco guitar and a classical" which Greek guitarists often prefer.

And what, you may be asking yourselves, do guitarists such as myself prefer? Well, my preference is for all of you to shift to your left one last time and join me at our final stop on this mornings' tour.....

MASA-TOSHI INOKUCHI

If you recall the beginning of the tour, I told you then that I had purposely chosen a member of the violin family of instruments to head the exhibition. I stated my reasons for doing so as being that most people have heard of Stradivari and that historically the most common image of instrument making has been the lone violin craftsman. It is not only for those reasons that I have intentionally brought you full circle, as it were, by concluding with a violin.

There is general agreement in the music world that the violin is the most perfectly designed acoustic instrument. Whether through luck or the fact of its lengthy developmental history, or both, the violin alone is felt to contain the perfect balance between tone qualities, volume, projection and user-friendly dimensions. Its physical proportions derive the maximum possible musical results from what is essentially,

as in most stringed instruments, a small but elaborate wooden box.

In addition, the violin produces sounds closer to the human voice than any other acoustic instrument, an ability given much credence by a world that deems the human in all its forms to be fine art's ultimate model.

So, do have these violin appreciations in mind as your guitar maker guide introduces you to the work of Mastoshi Inokuchi.

Masa, as his friends call him, built this violin primarily from Ontario woods. Regular searches throughout Ontario and the northeastern United States provide Masa with the curly maple and white spruce logs that his father-in-law and son help re-saw* into dimensioned, raw violin materials. Masa has found these more local species to equal the traditional European maples and spruces in producing good sounding instru-

Masa-toshi Inokuchi violin.
Canadian curly maple back, sides
and neck. Sitka spruce top.
58.7cm. x 21cm.

*see glossary

ments. It was our wood, in fact, that enticed him here from Japan in 1968.

Masa has been making instruments, violins and some guitars, professionally since 1958. His transition to a career as a luthier from teaching high school architecture and woodworking was, needless to say, an easy one. Books provided Masa with many of the basics of instrument construction, but the help of a guitar and violin making father-in-law proved an invaluable asset.

In the early years of self-instruction, Masa confided, he "felt the 'good' violin was out of reach". Whereas today, with his twenty-six years of accumulated knowledge, he radiates a mature confidence in his abilities and feels the good violins are not so difficult to build after all.

What did become a wearying difficulty for Masa after ten years as a maker was obtaining good materials. The superior woods always had to be imported into Japan at much expense and trouble. The solution as Masa saw it was to live nearer their source. That meant emigrating either to Germany, for their European curly maple, curly sycamore and German spruce, or to Canada for North American equivalents. I don't have to tell you which country he chose, but luckily for us, his first and last stop was Toronto.

Despite a schedule of violin making, that often sees the completion of two or three instruments in a month and the business of milling violin materials from logs that he and his son engage in, Masa still finds time to make profitable use of his architectural skills. He singlehandedly designed and constructed the interiors of many of the Japanese restaurants in Toronto, including the small eating establishment, Shoko Soba on Danforth Ave., owned by his wife Shoko and himself and run by her.

Masa's violins are constructed differently than most. Instead of the traditional joint that allows separation of the neck and body into two pieces, his necks remain integral parts of the bodies' construction. The neck and inner block on his violins are the same piece of wood into which recessed slots are cut to accept the ribs. This resembles a common style of classical guitar building that originated in Spain, known in the guitar world simply as Spanish Construction.

Like violin maker Anastas Fotev, Masa's dream is to build an entire string quartet: two violins, one viola and one cello. But Masa's vison goes one step further in that he would construct all four instruments from the wood of one log. Considering his sideline lumber ventures, it is an entirely possible goal.

We have reached the end of the tour.

I sincerely hope you have enjoyed yourselves and even learned a few things that you did'nt already know. You certainly have been a satisfying group to lead, what with all your good questions.

So, let me, in the name of all the artisans represented, thank you for coming and especially for patiently enduring my spieling for an entire morning.

If there are no more questions....Then, that's it, thank you again.

DEBORAH: Than YOU Mr. Laskin. You were very good.

LOUISE: Yes, thanks a lot. I'm sure I'll see you again though.

You are all very welcome!

GLOSSARY

ACTION — height of the strings in relation to the fingerboard.

ANHARMONICS, HARMONICS — audible dissonant and pleasing overtones respectively.

APPALACHIAN DULCIMER — a folk instrument common to the Appalachian mountain region of the U.S. It is usually a three or four string lap instrument.

ARCH-TOP — the term for a guitar with a top and back carved from thicker stock similar to violin family instruments.

BISQUE — in ceramics, the first kiln firing. Done before glazing to harden and dry the clay.

BOUT — the convex protrusions of an instrument's body.

DIATONIC — a standard major or minor musical scale of only eight notes to the octave.

EQUALIZING — in sound engineering, utilizing an electronic device to boost or cut certain chosen frequencies of the original sound.

FIFTHS — when tuned in fifths, each string is separated from the next higher by an interval of five notes. For example, between G and D occur five notes: G,A,B,C,D.

FINGERBOARD (FRETBOARD) — a strip of wood glued to the neck of a stringed instrument against which the strings are stopped.

FLAT-TOP — refers to guitars or mandolins whose top woods are thin, flat pieces reinforced with bracing.

FLUTING — a general descriptive term for decorative, rounded grooves.

FRENCH POLISHING — traditionally, the hand rubbed application of shellac to wood by means of a cotton or linen pad. Varnish or special "padding" lacquers often substitute for shellac.

FRETLESS — without raised fret markers of any type.

FROG — the moveable block at the heel of a violin bow to which the horsehair is attached.

GRAIN — in a musical instrument context: the surface appearance of the seasonal growth rings. The high density darker lines are the result of the tree's later summer growth. The low density wood in between resulted from the tree's early spring growth spurt.

JACK — the built in socket on an electric instrument's body into which the cord connecting the pickup electronics to the pre-amp or amplifier is inserted.

MANDRIL — a metal rod or bar used as a core around which metal, glass, clay etc. is moulded or shaped.

MOULDING — ornamental and/or functional shaped strips of wood.

NATURALS — on a keyboard instrument, the keys which play notes other than the sharps and flats. Generally: the 'white' keys.

NUT — a bar of ivory, bone, plastic, ebony or brass at the point where the fingerboard meets the peghead which serves to position the strings and hold them at the correct height above the frets.

PLATES — an alternate term for the top and back of a violin.

PRE-AMP. — an electronic device that amplifies a low level analog signal to a suitable level to drive an amplifier which in turn is capable of driving a speaker.

RE-SAW — further milling of raw lumber that has already been cut from the original log.

RIB — generally, the sides of a violin body or the strips of a lute bowl.

RING (GROWTH RING, ANNUAL RING) — the layer of wood added to a tree stem per yearly growth period.

ROUTED — hollowed out or gouged by means of a power tool known as a router.

SEMI-TONE — a "tone" at an interval of a half-step from another in a diatonic scale.

SOUNDBOARD — the top of a wooden, acoustic musical instrument. Labelled as such because of its major role in the instrument's production of sound.

THICKNESSING — reducing to a desired thickness (the dimension from surface to opposite surface) by removal of material.

TONE — a full interval between two notes of a diatonic scale.

TUNING MACHINES (MACHINE HEADS) — metal, geared string winding mechanisms for tuning.

BIBLIOGRAPHY

ALBARDA, JAN., H. — *Wood, Wire and Quill*, Toronto, 1975

ALZOFON, DAVID — "How Strings Are Made", Guitar Player, June 1983

BAINES, ANTHONY — *European And American Musical Instruments*, New York, 1966

BAINES, ANTHONY — *Catalogue Of Musical Instruments Volume II Non-Keyboard Instruments*, Victoria and Albert Museum, London, 1978

BAINES, ANTHONY ed. (various) — *Musical Instruments Through The Ages*, London, 1969

BARCLAY, ROBERT — "The Conservation Of Musical Instruments: A Case For Sentimental Value", Musicanada #48, Ottawa, May 1982

BLOOM, TONY and KETCHENSON, BLAIR — "Handmade Musical Instruments", Canada Crafts, Toronto, April/May, 1979

CHALIFOUX, SYLVAIN — "Organ Building In Canada: An Export Business," Musicanada #48, Ottawa, May 1982

EMERSON, MARILYN — "The Shock Of The New", The Strad volume 94 #1126, London 1984

EVANS, TOM AND MARY ANNE — *Guitars From The Renaissance To Rock*, London, 1977

FORD, CHARLES (VARIOUS) — *Making Musical Instruments, Strings And Keyboard*. New York, 1979

FRASER, EDMUND — *Practical Violin Making*, Atlanta, 1968

HAYDEN, NICK — "Tamburitzas," Guild of American Luthiers Data Sheet #18, Tacoma Washington, 1972

HAYES, FLORENCE — "Piano And Early Music Instruments In Canada," Musicanada #48, Ottawa, May 1982

HOADLY, BRUCE, R. — *Understanding Wood*, Newtown Conn. 1980

HUTCHINS, CARLEEN MALEY — "The Tuning Of Violin Plates," Scientific American Volume 245 #4, New York, 1981

JAFFRENNOU, GILDAS — *Folk Harps*, Hertshire, 1973

KALLMANN, HELMUT; POTVIN, GILLES; WINTERS, KENNETH; — *The Encyclopedia Of Music In Canada*, Toronto, 1981

MITCHELL BEAZLY PUBLISHERS — *The International Book of Wood*, New York, 1976

PAUL, JOHN — *Modern Harpsichord Makers*, London, 1981

PETRULIS, ROBERT, A. — "Basic Guitar Electronics," Guild Of American Luthiers Data Sheet #15, Tacoma Washington, 1972

POTVIN, GILLES — "Bowed String Instrument Making In Canada", Musicanada #48, Ottawa, May 1982

SLOANE, IRVING — *Steel String Guitar Construction*, New York, 1975

TURNBULL, HARVEY — *The Guitar From The Renaissance To The Present Day*, New York, 1974

WOODS, SLYVIA — *Teach Yourself To Play The Folk Harp*, Los Angeles, 1981

YOUNG, GAYLE — "Innovations In Instrument Design: The Excitement Of Discovery," Musicanada #48, Ottawa, May 1982